IMAGES OF WAR

ARMOURED WARFARE
IN THE
FAR EAST
1937–1945

A British M3 Lee medium tank and its happy looking crew on the banks of the Mu River near Chanta, Burma in January 1945. By this stage of the war morale was clearly high.

IMAGES OF WAR

ARMOURED WARFARE IN THE FAR EAST 1937–1945

RARE PHOTOGRAPHS FROM WARTIME ARCHIVES

Anthony Tucker-Jones

Pen & Sword
MILITARY

First published in Great Britain in 2015 by
PEN & SWORD MILITARY
an imprint of
Pen & Sword Books Ltd,
47 Church Street,
Barnsley,
South Yorkshire
S70 2AS

Text copyright © Anthony Tucker-Jones, 2015
Photographs copyright © as credited, 2015

Every effort has been made to trace the copyright of all the photographs.
If there are unintentional omissions, please contact the publisher in writing, who will correct all subsequent editions.

A CIP record for this book is available from the British Library.

ISBN 978 1 47385 167 2

The right of Anthony Tucker-Jones to be identified as Author of this Work has been asserted by him in accordance with the Copyright, Designs and Patents Act 1988.

All rights reserved. No part of this book may be reproduced or transmitted in any form or by any means, electronic or mechanical including photocopying, recording or by any information storage and retrieval system, without permission from the Publisher in writing.

Typeset by CHIC GRAPHICS

Printed and bound by CPI Group (UK) Ltd, Croydon, CR0 4YY

Pen & Sword Books Ltd incorporates the imprints of Pen & Sword Archaeology, Atlas, Aviation, Battleground, Discovery, Family History, History, Maritime, Military, Naval, Politics, Railways, Select, Social History, Transport, True Crime, Claymore Press, Frontline Books, Leo Cooper, Praetorian Press, Remember When, Seaforth Publishing and Wharncliffe.

For a complete list of Pen & Sword titles please contact
Pen & Sword Books Limited
47 Church Street, Barnsley, South Yorkshire, S70 2AS, England
E-mail: enquiries@pen-and-sword.co.uk
Website: www.pen-and-sword.co.uk

Contents

Introduction **7**

Photograph Sources **11**

Chapter One
    Tanks of the Rising Sun **12**

Chapter Two
    When Tigers Fight **25**

Chapter Three
    Mongolian Mayhem **38**

Chapter Four
    Khalkhin-Gol **47**

Chapter Five
    When Tigers Fight: The Sequel **58**

Chapter Six
    Fortress Singapore **68**

Chapter Seven
    Island Hopping **81**

Chapter Eight
Pacific Victory **95**

Chapter Nine
Jungles of Burma **105**

Chapter Ten
Assault on India **119**

Chapter Eleven
August Storm **131**

Chapter Twelve
Slow and Poorly Armed **136**

Introduction

On the very eve of the Second World War on the far side of the sprawling Soviet Union a largely unnoticed, short – but brutal – border war took place with Japan. Georgi Zhukov and his Red Army tanks inflicted such a devastating blow against the Imperial Japanese Army that it convinced Tokyo to look south for further territorial gains. Few in Europe had heard of Manchuria, let alone Mongolia, indeed at the time the world's attention was firmly focused on the fate of Czechoslovakia and Poland. In the Far East the long and bloody war between Japan and China was old news, as was Japan's creation of the puppet state of Manchukuo from prostrate Manchuria. So some distant border clash between the USSR and Japan seemed of little consequence to Europe's diplomats fretting over avoiding war with Hitler's resurgent Germany. The Japanese were taught a highly valuable lesson at the hands of the Red Army about armoured warfare, but crucially they failed to heed it.

On 7 December 1941, Japan struck at Pearl Harbor; the next day Japanese forces occupied Shanghai and Siam (Thailand) and landed in British Malaya. Trundling down the roads through Malaya's rubber plantations came Japanese light and medium tanks. These caused chaos and panic and swiftly overran British defences. At Muar Australian anti-tank gunners put up a highly spirited defence but it was to no avail. Twenty-four hours after the invasion of Malaya the Imperial Japanese Navy sank two British battleships, the *Repulse* and the *Prince of Wales*, crippling Britain's naval strength in the Pacific in one fell swoop. Japan reigned supreme in the air and at sea. On the ground the Japanese Blitzkrieg continued this trend.

Just after the attack on Pearl Harbor the Japanese captured the American island of Guam. In the New Year they attacked the Philippines with tanks spearheading the assault on Luzon. British Hong Kong fell to the Japanese in late December 1941. Shortly after having been driven from Malaya British forces at Singapore surrendered in February 1942. The following month the Japanese occupied most of Java, Sumatra and other islands of the Dutch East Indies. In Burma British and Chinese troops were swiftly driven back toward the Indian border. An Imperial Tokyo communiqué announced on 9 March 1942 that Rangoon, the capital of Burma, had been seized. This threatened India and China's western frontier. Japanese tanks then helped humiliate American and Filipino troops trapped at Bataan.

The fighting in China, South-East Asia and the Pacific during the 1930s and 1940s is not generally known for its armoured or mechanised warfare. Nevertheless a wide range of regular armed forces employed armoured vehicles to varying degrees during the various campaigns fought in the Far East and the Pacific, including the American, Australian, British, Chinese, Indian, Russian and Japanese armies. Renegade proxy forces such as the semi-independent Japanese Kwantung Army and the puppet Chinese Manchukuo Imperial Army also deployed tanks.

In all these operations Japanese tanks played a part. Whereas tanks such as the Sherman, Panther, Tiger, T-34 and others have gone down in history as key pieces of equipment, the Japanese *Chi-Ha*, *Ha-Go* and *I-Go* are little known outside military circles. In particular the Type 97 *Chi-Ha* was the most widely deployed Japanese medium tank of the Second World War but over the years it has gained little fame or notoriety. Once the war began to go against Japan, the priority for aircraft and warships to defend the Japanese homeland ensured that its tank fleet was never very large compared to those of the Western armies.

Geography also played its role in the evolution of armoured warfare in this part of the world. Perhaps understandably at the time, the jungles of Burma, Malaya and Thailand and the coral islands of the Pacific were considered wholly unsuitable tank country. Events were to prove otherwise, but this initial mindset stifled the use of armour.

In contrast the open spaces of Manchuria seemed ideal, but Japanese tanks encountered few Chinese counterparts. Despite being flat, conditions were far from perfect as there were vast areas of marshes and flood plain that were not suitable for vehicles during the wet season. In addition the fertile Manchurian Plain, also known as the North-East China Plain, is very hot during the summer and bitterly cold in the winter. The Japanese came to the conclusion that their existing tanks were fit for purpose and this mentality continued until the very end of the Second World War.

The political complexity of the wars fought in the Far East far outweighed the multinational campaigns fought in North Africa, Italy, France and indeed Russia. In the case of the latter, Germany and Italy were the common enemy. In the Far East all the players had competing goals and alliances of convenience were strained and often short lived. China's Nationalist government was fighting to maintain and extend central authority, while China's Communists were seeking regime change. Although opposed to each other, both were united in their opposition to Japanese aggression on the Chinese mainland. Caught in the middle were China's powerful warlords who maintained strong provincial militias that sided with whoever was in the ascendancy. These militias were often at best simply police forces intent on keeping law and order – at worst they were bandits who terrorised the civilian population and took what they wanted.

At the same time Japanese forces in China and Korea were seeking to hold and gain additional Chinese territory. These were supported by collaborationist Chinese and Korean forces that had little option but to cooperate with their colonial masters. Again the latter were little more than militias who normally lacked heavy equipment. Meanwhile the Soviet Union, having tangled with both China and Japan in the 1930s, sought to avoid further war while it concentrated on events unfolding in Europe.

Fighting in China was inevitably shaped by its sheer size, the Chinese Nationalists needed to hold ground which required large standing armies, while the Communists, short of equipment, resorted to guerrilla warfare to achieve their goals. The one thing that China was not short of was manpower and this was reflected in the doctrinal thinking of the Chinese military. Despite advances in technology and lessons from the First World War, they preferred to rely on weight of numbers.

Like the Chinese, the Japanese – although swift to embrace the merits of artillery and aircraft – were much slower than European armies to adapt to the requirements of armoured and mechanised warfare. The Japanese only created four armoured divisions and one of these never saw action. The first three were only formed in 1942 in Manchuria and the fourth created two years later was intended for the defence of the Japanese homeland. As a result there were no large-scale tank battles to rival as El Alamein, Kursk or Normandy.

Nonetheless, until the British and American Burma and Pacific Campaigns, Japanese tank forces largely had it their own way. Crucially the Japanese put their tanks to good use against the Chinese and subsequently were a key factor for the Japanese success in capturing Malaya and Singapore from the poorly led British forces.

In the opening stages of the Second World War in the Pacific, American light tanks did nothing to stave off America's defeat in the Philippines. American light tank crews arrived on Luzon ill prepared to fight armoured warfare against the Japanese. The Stuart tank found itself bested by the Japanese Type 97 and the small American tank force was soon lost during the retreat to Bataan. Once the American-built Lee and Sherman medium tanks entered the fray, Japanese tanks became obsolete overnight.

Stuart, Grant and Sherman tanks were called upon to perform a wide variety of combat missions in both the Far East and Pacific, ranging from acting as mobile pillboxes to bunker busting. In Burma they were employed to knock out enemy positions, scale steep defended hills and clear trees for advancing troops. Japanese anti-tank guns, anti-tank mines and artillery ensured that the advance of enemy tanks was severely contested. On the whole British tanks were utilised in their more traditional role of infantry support – it was only during the Imphal-Kohima and Meiktila-Mandalay battles that anything like true mechanised warfare was waged against the Japanese.

American tanks provided an advantage but certainly not a decisive one once operations commenced to drive the Japanese back across the Pacific. In many places the medium tanks were simply too heavy and so troops relied on light tanks to provide support. Despite the massive resources of the US Fleet and the US Marine Corps, once a tank crew was ashore it was pretty much on its own. Often on the confines of the small atolls tanks provided tempting and vulnerable targets for Japanese gunners. In the Pacific, US tank crews sweltered inside their tanks enduring heat exhaustion, dehydration and malaria.

The Japanese were expert at burrowing into the volcanic hills and mountains that covered the larger islands. These they these turned into natural fortresses with hidden gun positions and connecting subterranean passageways. Such defensive positions created deadly interconnecting fields of fire that dominated the exits off the beaches and inland. Nearer the beaches they created log bunkers using felled palm trees packed with coral and sand. These were protected by mines, anti-tank ditches and heavy artillery and proved highly resilient. Where naval gunfire and dive-bombers failed to silence Japanese strongpoints, tanks and flame-throwers were called upon to smash them open at point-blank range. Often the Japanese continued to battle on way beyond the point at which resistance had become futile.

Shermans supporting US infantry and marines found that before they even reached the beaches they had to negotiate reefs and treacherous shallows that could suddenly swallow a wading tank. Even when the crew managed to escape they found themselves running the deadly gauntlet of enemy fire raking the water and the shoreline. Like the beaches themselves, these shallows were obstructed by obstacles and covered by large-calibre guns and mines. Quite often for the opening attack the Americans had to rely on their amphibious tractors – or Amtracs – which were progressively up-armoured and up-gunned as the war progressed.

Those Japanese tanks supporting the island garrisons were rarely used in a conventional manner. Limited Japanese armoured operations using inadequate tanks on Guam and Peleliu were simply killed in their tracks. More often than not they were buried in coral and basalt and turned into pillboxes that would spray the unwary in machine-gun and shellfire. After the war, numbers of Japanese tanks were seized intact not only on the Japanese mainland but also on the islands that had been bypassed by the amphibious operations.

Photograph Sources

The dramatic images in this volume have been drawn principally from those taken by the American combat photographers who served with the US Marine Corps and US Army's Signal Corps in the Pacific. These are now held by the US National Archives and Records Administration (NARA) and the quality of the photographers' work speaks for itself. Many are also drawn from the author's own extensive collection. Lastly the author is indebted to a number of individuals who were kind enough to share their private collections and offer their expertise.

Chapter One

Tanks of the Rising Sun

The perception of the Japanese Imperial Army during the Second World War is one of brutality, massed banzai infantry charges and kamikaze suicide pilots. Certainly the Japanese armed forces were far from mechanised and what armour and artillery they did develop during the 1930s – while practical – was fairly rudimentary. However, until the Japanese briefly came up against the Russians in 1939 in Mongolia and the Americans in 1942 in the Pacific, their enemies had not been greatly mechanised either. Notably when Japan went to war with China in 1937, the Chinese Army comprised mainly infantry divisions.

Despite it being reasonably good tank country, the Japanese Kwantung Army stationed in Manchuria had surprisingly few dedicated armoured units with which to fight the Chinese, or indeed the Soviets. In 1937 these amounted to just two armoured brigades (1st Tank with 3rd Army and 2nd Armoured with 4th Army). There were also two tank training regiments (23rd and 24th) overseen by the 1st Tank Army training school. Two years later, the 3rd and 4th Tank regiments constituted the armoured Yasuoka Task Force involved in the Nomonhan Incident – or the Battle of Khalkhin-Gol – with the Red Army. In light of the effectiveness of Soviet armour at Khalkhin-Gol and other border clashes, it is surprising that a greater effort was not made to develop the tank units of the Japanese and Chinese Manchukuo forces.

It was not until the Japanese attack on Pearl Harbor that these forces were enhanced with the creation of Taku (Development) 1st Armoured Group with three tank regiments at Poli, Manchuria, drawing on the 1st Tank Brigade and Geki (Hit) 2nd Armoured Group at Mutangchiang, Manchuria, also with four tank regiments. These units were not redesignated as divisions until mid-1942. Inevitably many of the better Kwantung units were redeployed for operations against the Americans in the Pacific.

The Manchukuo Imperial Army had a number of armoured cars built by Isuzu and modified by the Dowa Automobile Company of Manchukuo, but little else. From 1943, some ten Type 94 tankettes were passed to the Manchukuo Army to form one armoured company. During the war, a Manchukuo version of the Japanese

Type 95 *Ha-Go* was in used in training tank schools, but did not reach substantial operational deployment.

Elsewhere in China there was a myriad different competing armed forces, including the National Revolutionary Army (NRA), the Communist armies and the private armies of various regional warlords. The National Revolutionary Army of the Republic of China was the military arm of the Kuomintang (KMT, or the Chinese Nationalist Party). The NRA had few dedicated armoured and mechanised units. It never became a great proponent of armoured or mechanised warfare, preferring instead to rely on numbers supported by artillery and, where possible, aircraft.

NRA tank forces remained limited throughout the Second Sino-Japanese War of 1937–45. At the start of this conflict these were organised into just three armoured battalions, equipped with an assortment of tanks and armoured cars supplied by various countries. A single mechanised division was formed, but its armoured and artillery regiments were placed under command of the 5th Army, while the division became a motorised infantry division within the same army. The latter fought battles in Guangxi in 1939–40 and in the Battle of Yunnan-Burma Road in 1942, again reducing the armored unit's strength due to losses and mechanical breakdowns. Late in the Burma Campaign, the NRA forces committed to the fighting there had an armoured battalion equipped with Sherman tanks.

During the Second Sino-Japanese War, the Communist military forces were nominally integrated into the NRA, forming the 8th Route Army and the New 4th Army units. During this time, these two military groups primarily used guerrilla warfare and fought a few battles with the Japanese, while consolidating their ground by annexing nationalist troops and paramilitary forces behind the Japanese lines.

By the late 1930s Japan's principal tank types were the Type 89B *Ot-Su* and Type 97 *Chi-Ha* medium tanks and the Type 95 *Ha-Go* light tank. Numbers of the largely obsolete Type 94/92 and Type 97 *Te-Ke/Ke-Ke* tankettes were also in use. Notably the former was based on the British Carden-Loyd Mk VI, but was eventually replaced by the Type 97.

The Japanese Osaka Arsenal copied the British Vickers Medium C to produce the Type 89 tank, which was developed into a four-man medium tank in 1929. A 12.8-ton version known as the Type 89B, armed with a 57mm gun and built by Mitsubishi, went into service in the mid-1930s and served with the Japanese Army for almost a decade. Likewise the 7-ton Type 95 appeared in the mid-1930s and was armed with a 37mm gun and had a three-man crew. This proved to be the most-utilised Japanese small tank seeing action first in China and then throughout the Far East during the Second World War.

The Type 97 medium tank, armed with a short-barrelled 57mm gun, was one of the most successful Japanese tank designs, though it was to prove no match for the

American Sherman or Grant. This was a scaled-up version of the Type 95, and although twice the weight at 14.8 tons, it was quite fast and could manage 24mph – almost the same speed as its predecessor. An improved version, armed with a high-velocity 47mm gun, known as the *Shinhoto Chi-Ha*, did not appear until 1942.

During the fighting in Burma and India the British M3 Grant tanks, redeployed from North Africa where they had been outclassed by later German panzers, were more than a match for Japanese armour. The Type 1 *Ho-Ni 1* self-propelled gun (based on the Type 97 chassis), armed with a Type 90 75mm field gun, was the only Japanese armoured fighting vehicle capable of knocking out American-built tanks. A version mounting the Type 90 gun in a turret was also produced as the Type 3 *Chi-Nu*, but in very limited numbers from 1943 onwards. Self-propelled artillery was provided in the shape of the Type 4 *Ho-Ro*, mounting a 150mm howitzer.

With the arrival of the Sherman, Japan's tanks were rendered almost completely obsolete. In the Pacific, Japanese tanks tended to act as pillboxes, but remained vulnerable to fighter-bombers, naval gunfire and American armour. Towards the end of the war the Type 4 *Chi-To* and Type 5 *Chi-Ri* medium tanks did not get much beyond the design stage. A few Type 4s were built and deployed for defence of the Japanese homeland, while only a prototype Type 5 was produced. If it had gone into production armed with a 75mm gun and with 75mm of armour, it would have been a difficult nut to crack. However, by this stage, the powerful American M26 Pershing had been deployed to the Pacific.

During the Second World War the Japanese Army deployed four large-calibre anti-tank weapons; two were 37mm semi-automatics, the third was a 70mm light howitzer and the fourth an obsolete 75mm pack artillery field piece. The oldest, based on the US 37mm-gun M1916, entered service in 1922 as the Type 11 low-trajectory Infantry Support Gun. It fired the Type 12 high-explosive shell as well as an ineffective anti-tank shell. Its role was to deal with enemy machine-gun positions and light tanks, and in a modified form was used to arm some early Japanese tanks (the Japanese Renault NC27 and early Type 89 *I-Go* medium tanks). It was largely superseded by the Type 94 37mm anti-tank gun by the beginning of the Pacific War.

The Type 11 was effective in the early stages of the Second-Sino-Japanese War, providing heavy fire support against semi-fortified positions, such as pillboxes, machine-gun nests and lightly armored vehicles. In contrast, its low muzzle velocity, small calibre and low rate of fire, ensured that it was obsolete against Allied forces equipped with medium tanks. As a result it was not issued outside of reserve units during the Pacific War.

The rapid-fire Type 94 37mm infantry gun introduced in 1934 was a light semi-automatic, with a split trail wheeled carriage making it look like a small field gun. To present a lower silhouette, the Type 94 had a removable single-piece armour plate shield. This gun proved wholly unsatisfactory against Soviet tanks in 1939 and was upgraded with a longer barrel to create the Type 1 37mm anti-tank gun. This was eventually supplemented by the Type 1 47mm anti-tank gun.

The Type 97 was known by the Japanese Army as the RA 97 (the RA standing for Reinmetaru – Japanese for Rheinmettal). This was because the gun was the German 37mm Panzer Abwehr Kanone 37, manufactured by Rheinmettal-Borsig and exported to Japan in some numbers in 1937–39.

Initially the Type 1 47mm was assumed to be an enlarged 37mm. However, it is more likely that it was based on the Soviet ZIK 45mm anti-tank gun. Ironically the latter was little more than an enlarged copy of the Rheinmettal design, as these had also been sold to the Soviets in 1936–37. It is likely that the Japanese laid their hands on the Soviet 45mm gun following the Manchurian border clashes with Soviet troops in 1938–39.

The Type 92 howitzer was a small and mobile 70mm calibre weapon consisting of a short, stubby barrel on a steel disc-wheeled, split-trail carriage. The Meiji 41st Year type 75mm regimental gun was introduced to the pack artillery in 1908 and was issued to the infantry in the mid-1930s after being replaced in the pack artillery role by the 75mm Type 94 mountain gun. It was the first Japanese weapon to be supplied in 1940 with hollow charge anti-tank ammunition.

Japanese infantry were also equipped with the Type 97 anti-tank rifle that fired a powerful 20mm cartridge, but it was disliked owing to its heavy recoil. The bullets could pierce 15mm of face-hardened armour plate at 200m. The Type 98 light anti-aircraft gun, which appeared on single or twin mounts, was a larger and heavier version of the anti-tank rifle. Its longer and wider cartridge used the same projectile as the Type 97 and was used as an anti-tank weapon mounted on a small-wheeled carriage. Other infantry anti-tank weapons included the Type 3 anti-tank grenade (though these may not have been introduced until the early 1940s) and the Type 99 magnetised anti-tank mine. Later pole-mounted lunge mines used in suicide attacks could penetrate up to 150mm of plate armour.

A local-built variant of the French Hotchkiss 25mm anti-aircraft gun known as the Type 96 was used by the Imperial Japanese Navy during the Second World War. While it was primarily used as an anti-aircraft gun in fixed mounts with between one and three guns, it was also designed as a dual-purpose weapon for use against armoured vehicles. While not ideal, many of these weapons ensured that the Japanese could hold their own against Western armies on numerous occasions.

After the First World War the Japanese obtained about a dozen British-built Whippet tanks to form a fledgling armoured force. These were photographed in Manchuria in the 1930s.

Japanese medium tank designs were initially not very successful. Experimental Tank No. 1 was the basis for the Japanese Type 89 medium tank; it drew on the British Medium C which the Japanese Army obtained in 1927.

The Japanese Type 89 medium tank, armed with a 57mm gun, first went into production in 1931. This is an early model Type 89A *I-Go Kō*, of which 220 were built, followed by 189 of the Type 89B *I-Go Otsu*. Armed with a Type 90 57mm gun and two machine-guns (one in the hull and one in the rear of the turret), the *I-Go* had a maximum of 17mm of armour. Like most of the tanks of its day it was not very fast, managing 17mph with a range of just 100 miles (160km) and was powered by a Mitsubishi six-cylinder diesel engine.

This is either a late model *I-Go Kō* or the subsequent *I-Go Otsu*. The size of the turret and the location of the hull machine-gun indicate the former. Although the *I-Go* had a four-man crew, the commander had to act as the gunner, supported by a loader. The *I-Go* saw combat in the Second Sino-Japanese War, at Khalkhin-Gol against the Red Army and in the Second World War.

The Type 92 heavy armoured car went into production in 1932 but proved wholly unsatisfactory and so only 167 had been built by 1939. Although actually a tracked light tank, as the Type 92 was intended for the cavalry, it was dubbed an armoured car because tanks came under the control of the infantry. It was mainly deployed in Manchuria and Korea.

The Japanese experimented with a twin-turret heavy tank dubbed the Type 95, armed with 70mm and 37mm guns, but this went no further than the prototype stage in 1934.

The two-man Type 94 tankette entered service in the mid-1930s. While only armed with a machine-gun and with just 12mm of armour, it was quite effective against the Chinese National Revolutionary Army. It was followed by the up-gunned Type 97 *Te-Ke* tankette armed with a 37mm gun.

Type 97 *Te-Ke*, which entered service in 1935, was a two-man tankette armed with a Type 94 37mm gun, but no machine-gun. In some models the 37mm gun was replaced with a 7.7mm machine-gun. It only had a maximum of 12mm of armour to protect the crew.

The Type 95 *Ha-Go* light tank went into production in 1936 and over 2,000 were built. It required three crew (a commander/gunner, hull machine-gunner and driver) and was armed with a turret-mounted Type 94 37mm gun and a hull-mounted Type 91 6.5mm machine-gun. The maximum thickness of the armour was just 12mm. Its diesel engine gave a top road speed of 28mph with a combat range of 156 miles (250km). The *Ha-Go* saw action during the Second Sino-Japanese War, at Nomonhan, against the Red Army and in the Second World War.

In 1943 the Japanese produced the Type 1 *Chi-He* medium tank, which was an upgrade of the Type 97. As the Japanese Navy was given priority over steel production, only 170 Type 1s were built and most of these were deployed to defend the Japanese home islands.

The Type 97 *Chi-Ha* was the most widely produced Japanese medium tank of the Second World War. Between 1938 and 1943 over 2,100 were constructed. Initially it was armed with a short 57mm gun and with up to 28mm of armour, but from 1942 the *Kai Shinhoto Chi-Ha* variant was equipped with a long-barrelled 47mm gun that gave a much higher muzzle velocity.

The Type 2 *Ho-I* support tank was a heavily armed variant of the Type 97. This was equipped with a Type 41 75mm mountain gun to provide support against enemy fortified positions. By 1944 just 30 conversions had been made and mass production never started. These were deployed to defend Japan.

To counter the US M4 Sherman, the Japanese developed the Type 3 *Chi-Nu* in 1943 but it did not go into production until the following year. Only 144 were built and these remained in Japan.

Japanese anti-tank weapons included the Type 94 light semi-automatic infantry gun introduced in 1934 that served as the Imperial Japanese Army's standard 37mm anti-tank gun.

The Japanese Type 11 37mm infantry gun came into service in 1922 and was initially used in the Type 89 *I-Go* medium tank. This weapon could tackle lightly armoured vehicles, but certainly not the Allies' medium tanks.

Chapter Two

When Tigers Fight

Troubled Japanese and Chinese relations came to a head in 1894 when they fought bitterly over control of Korea in the First Sino-Japanese War. The outcome was the Treaty at Shimonoseki, in which China abandoned her rights to Korea, ceding not only the Laiodong Peninsula in the north, but also Formosa (Taiwan) and the Pescadore Islands, along with an indemnity of $200 million. At the start of the First World War, Japan was swift to seize all of Germany's interests in the region. In 1915 the Twenty-One Demands saw China cede all Germany's regional rights to Tokyo, effectively making China a Japanese protectorate.

Chiang Kai-Shek formed a Nationalist government – the Kuomintang (KMT) – in 1927, but his dictatorial regime was opposed by Mao Tse Tung's Communists and numerous warlords. Civil war erupted in 1930, seriously weakening the country. The following year Japan, with an eye on China's vast natural resources, took advantage of the situation and invaded and occupied Manchuria. The Japanese created a nominally independent state called Manchukuo, but the Chinese Emperor who ruled it was little more than a Japanese puppet. From their Manchurian base the Japanese continued to encroach on Chinese territory and the whole of northern China was gradually taken over.

Chiang Kai-Shek's strategy was first to secure full control of China by defeating the Communists and to then turn his attention to the defence of the frontier. This policy played into the hands of the Japanese. Ultimately it was only a matter of time before open conflict broke out once again between the two countries. In 1937 Japanese forces, exercising in the Lugouqiao area near the Marco Polo Bridge, discovered one of their men missing. Although he returned two hours later, the Japanese demanded the Chinese garrison commander of Wanping (ironically meaning 'obliging peace') allow them to search the town. He refused and the Japanese sought to use this to improve their position in northern China. As a pretext for war they demanded that the Chinese 29th Army withdraw from all strategic areas.

The British novelist J.G. Ballard, who was born and raised in Shanghai in the 1930s, noted: 'For the first time in the history of warfare a coordinated air, sea and land assault was launched against Chiang Kai-Shek's Chinese armies, who greatly outnumbered the Japanese, but were poorly led by corrupt cronies of Chiang and his wife.'

The Japanese Shanghai Expeditionary Army marched on the city on 22 August 1937 supported by Type 89, 94 and 95 tanks. Each infantry division had a tankette company which had six Type 94s employed in a reconnaissance role. Shanghai was no place for armour, but this did not stop both sides deploying it on the streets. Shortly after fighting broke out in Shanghai, a Chinese counter-attack against the well-fortified Japanese concession was thwarted by Japanese tanks.

In the early part of the three-month battle for Shanghai, the Chinese committed their fledgling tank force in an all-out attempt to destroy the small and beleaguered Japanese enclave. China's main weapon was the British-built Vickers export Mark E medium tank. The Chinese had imported around 20 in the years prior to the battle of Shanghai; the Type A had two turrets, but the Chinese opted for Type B variant, which featured a single turret equipped with a powerful short-barrelled 47mm gun and a machine-gun. It was part of an ambitious weapons procurement programme initiated by a Chinese government convinced that war with Japan was inevitable.

These tanks were foolishly used to attack the almost impenetrable Japanese positions. These were defended by guns, bombers and the powerful naval artillery of the Japanese Third Fleet, anchored just a few hundred yards away in Shanghai's Huangpu River. The Chinese tank crews were further disadvantaged by lack of coordination with the supporting infantry. This situation left the tanks exposed. Shanghai's streets were a terrible place in which to wage a tank battle, as the Japanese also came to realise.

On 18 August 1937 the Chinese decided to send the newly arrived 36th Division into the fray, attacking the Hueishan docks on the northern side of the Huangpu River. Meanwhile, the 87th Division broke through Japanese lines at Yangshupu, and pushed onto the Hueishan docks along with the 36th Division. On 22 August, the tanks of the 36th Division reached the docks, but were not able to hold the position for long. The Chinese troops were insufficiently trained in coordinating infantry–tank tactics, and the troops were unable to keep up with the tanks. Without sufficient infantry to protect them, the tanks were vulnerable to Japanese anti-tank weapons and artillery in close quarters and became useless when they entered the city centre. The few troops who did manage to keep up with the tanks through the city blocks were then trapped by Japanese blockades and annihilated by flame-throwers and intense machine-gun fire. The Vickers tanks therefore failed because of flawed tactics rather than any technical issues.

'The Chinese pushed the Japanese back towards the river, until they were fighting in trenches that filled with water at high tide. But the Japanese prevailed, and

Chiang's armies withdrew into the vast interior of China. [After Nanking] The new national capital became Chungking, 900 miles to the west,' recalled J.G. Ballard.

The Chinese fielded about 450,000 troops, although only 80,000 were equipped with modern German weapons and 60 per cent of these were lost trying to save Shanghai. Critically they also lost 10,000 well-trained junior officers. Only at Taierzhuang did the Japanese suffer a reverse when 20,000 of their troops were killed or wounded in the worst defeat ever suffered by the Japanese Army. This convinced them that there would be no quick victory in China.

Following the fall of Shanghai, Chiang Kai-Shek doubted the ability of his remaining troops to hold his capital Nanking in the face of renewed Japanese attack. The city lay just 186 miles west of Shanghai. He preferred to preserve his best troops and withdraw into China's vast interior where he could wear down the Japanese. Nonetheless, he still decided to fight at Nanking, needlessly sacrificing units that should have been saved for another day. There were to be no tank battles, but armour from both sides played its part. Chiang flew to Wuhan, leaving behind General Tang Shengzhi with 100,000 ill-trained and dispirited troops. When units fleeing from Shanghai began to pass through the area, morale all but collapsed.

After suffering heavy casualties taking Shanghai, the Japanese were reluctant to renew their offensive, but then on 1 December 1937, Tokyo ordered the Central China Area Army to take Nanking. This numbered well over 160,000, although only a third would be committed to the fighting for the city. In reality they were already on their way. The Central China Area Army launched a two-pronged attack with the 10th Army marching on Nanking from the south and the Shanghai Expeditionary Army (SEA) moving in from the east. To the north and west Japanese forces were moved into position to block escape routes over the Yangtze River.

Thanks to their tanks and air supremacy, the Japanese swiftly overcame those retreating Chinese units that were foolish enough to stand in their way. The Chinese defensive strategy was flawed in that their forces exposed themselves to air attack and artillery fire by holding high ground, which was easily outflanked by the Japanese tanks and surrounded. By 5 December the city was within range of the Japanese artillery. The SEA pierced Nanking's outer defences after overcoming a spirited defence by the Chinese 51st Division. To the south, the armour of the Japanese 10th Army overwhelmed the Chinese 58th Division. On 9 December the advancing Japanese, having reached the city's last line of defence, called on the defenders to surrender within 24 hours.

After receiving no response, the Japanese – under the cover of artillery and aerial bombardment – stormed the city's defences. When the Japanese breached the walls, the Chinese counter-attacked with tanks but they were driven off by Japanese artillery fire. The 10th Army stormed the Yuhuatai plateau to the south, which had been fortified with trenches and pillboxes held by three Chinese divisions, including the German-trained 88th Division. The latter fought to the last, but Yuhuatai was overrun by midday on 12 December. One Chinese tank unit fleeing the chaos had to charge their own side to reach the harbour at Xiaguan, only to find there were too few boats to take the crowds desperate to escape over the Yangtze.

Japanese operations were not renewed until October 1938 (by which time the Type 97 medium tank and tankette were entering service) when Wuhan was captured. In the meantime the Chinese had moved their defence industries out of harm's way. Although Japan's mechanised forces kept breaking through Chinese lines, the latter's superiority of numbers meant the Japanese could never achieve total victory.

By the following year the Japanese had 25 divisions tied down in eastern China. However, another 14 divisions and two air groups were in Manchuria and Korea, with another seven garrisoning Japan and Taiwan. Although more men would be mobilised for the war in the Pacific, those forces in China were not substantially reinforced in 1939–41.

Notably all these Japanese operations were conducted with second-line reserves with only a few units from Manchukuo. The best troops were held back for an attack on the Soviet Union – certainly the consolidation of Japanese military might in northern China and Inner Mongolia seemed to indicate that this was the case. The last thing they wanted to do was divert their 300,000 troops to central China.

Following the loss of the NRA's tank units during the battles of Shanghai and Nanking, new tanks, armoured cars and trucks supplied by the Soviet Union and Italy made it possible to form the NRA's only mechanised division, designated the 200th Division. It was equipped with Soviet T-26 light tanks and BT-5 fast tanks, but ceased to be a mechanised unit after the June 1938 reorganisation of the NRA.

In June 1940 the Russo-Japanese dispute was settled with a border treaty and 12 months later Hitler attacked the Soviet Union. Following the Japan-Soviet ceasefire, the Japanese – content that the Red Army was fully distracted – renewed the war in China with 100,000 men massed in northern Hunan. The war had been a series of set-piece battles, but after 1939 it became a series of bloody brawls, which would drag on throughout the Second World War. Subsequent fighting involving Chinese forces stretched from Burma in the far west to the Soviet Union in the far north-east.

Japanese troops entering Qiqihar in 1931 following the Mukden Incident. There would be another six years of provocation by Tokyo before the Second Sino-Japanese War broke out.

Motorised Japanese troops in Manchuria in 1931. They easily cut through the weak Chinese armies in the region. At this stage the Japanese were still in the process of developing their tank force in the shape of the Type 89 medium tank and the Type 92 'armoured car'.

Japanese troops fighting in Inner Mongolia in 1933. The Japanese seized the province of Rehe from a Chinese warlord and added it to their puppet state of Manchukuo.

Type 89s on the move somewhere in China. The middle tank is the initial model Type 89A *I-Go Kō*, while the others are improved Type 89As which include a commander's cupola as well as the single shallow-sloped frontal armour plate which offered more protection for the driver. Notably, though, the hull machine-guns remain on the right as was the case in the earlier model.

The Type 94 tankette was just about adequate for fighting the Chinese. Nevertheless it was found to throw its tracks when doing high-speed turns, so this led to the development of a larger idler wheel at the rear that touched the ground – visible on this late model.

The Japanese Type 4 150mm howitzer was a First World War-vintage weapon, but continued to be employed during the Sino-Japanese War and the Second World War.

The Japanese Type 96 dual-mounted 25mm anti-aircraft gun first came into service in the mid-1930s and could also be deployed in an anti-tank role.

Japanese troops with the Type 11 light machine-gun. This came into service in 1922 and was the standard LMG to see combat during the Manchurian Incident and in the early stages of the Second Sino-Japanese War. Although superseded by the Type 96 in the mid-1930s, it continued in frontline use during the Second World War.

Chinese Nationalist leader Chiang Kai-Shek, whose forces were known as the National Revolutionary Army.

The NRA was largely an infantry army.

These Nationalist Chinese troops, wearing German-supplied helmets, are firing a French-supplied Hotchkiss light machine-gun in an anti-aircraft role.

A National Revolutionary Army howitzer. Chiang Kai-Shek had very few tank forces and these were unsuccessfully committed to the defence of Shanghai.

Japanese naval infantry fighting on the streets of Shanghai in 1937. They are supported by a Type 11 light machine-gun.

Chinese Vickers tanks captured by the Japanese during the Battle for Shanghai. Thanks to the poor showing of China's tank force, the Japanese remained convinced that their tank designs were adequate.

Japanese Type 94 tanks attacking Nanking. By 1936 each Japanese infantry division was supported by a tankette company equipped with six Type 94s. Around 750 were built during the mid-1930s.

A Japanese tank crew surveys the debris of war scattered along Nanking's Zhongshan Road in December 1937.

Suspicious Japanese troops searching for Chinese troops masquerading as civilians in Nanking Castle.

Chapter Three

Mongolian Mayhem

A decade after the Treaty at Shimonoseki, Japan turned on Imperial Russia, attacking its fleet at Port Arthur (Lüda) in 1904, taking over the latter and gaining Russia's rights in the southern part of Manchuria. The humiliation of Russia's forces in 1904 and 1905 ensured that simmering resentment marred their relations throughout the 1920s and 1930s. After the Japanese occupation of Korea and Manchuria, friction between Japan and the Soviet Union was inevitable.

The main Japanese force in Manchukuo was the Kwantung Army, which in 1939 contained some of the Imperial Japanese Army's best units. In particular, western Manchukuo was garrisoned by the 23rd Division under General Michitarō Komatsubara, based at Hailar. The principal Soviet formation in the region was the 57th Special Corps, forward-deployed from the Trans-Baikal Military District.

Japan had an eye on Vladivostok, but to keep the Red Army at bay the Japanese would need to sever the Trans-Siberian railway. However, the Japanese military had always been divided over a 'Strike South' at the Western powers' colonial interests or a 'Strike North' against Russia. The Soviets took the opportunity of seizing the tactically important Changkufeng Hill near the mouth of the Tyumen River on the eastern border south-west of Vladivostok to protect the port.

Throughout the summer of 1938 the Japanese probed Russian defences with a series of border incidents near Vladivostok at Lake Khasan. The Soviet response was poor, revealing the true extent of Stalin's purges of the Red Army during the 1930s. Indeed, Russian General Lyushkov defected to the Kwantung Army, telling the Japanese exactly what they wanted to hear.

Acting without Emperor Hirohito's knowledge or permission, the Kwantung Army struck. On 11 July 1938 fighting broke out when the Japanese tried to remove the Russians from Changkufeng, however they had fortified the area and remained in possession of the hill following an armistice on 10 August. Soviet armour and air power put an end to early success, and Hirohito, on being informed of what was happening, refused to allow the Japanese Air Force to support the Army.

The Imperial Japanese Army now faced losing face with the formal ceasefire at Lake Khasan, however Hirohito agreed to the General Staff's plan to act further west against Outer Mongolia (Inner Mongolia belonged to China). The latter was tied to the USSR by a mutual assistance pact dating back to March 1936, but the Japanese no doubt hoped that the Red Army would be too stretched to intervene effectively.

The Kwantung Army selected an area beside the Khalkhin-Gol River, as this formed much of the boundary between Manchukuo to the east and the Outer Mongolian Peoples' Republic to the west. The Japanese claimed that the border was the Khalkhin-Gol River, while in contrast the Mongolians and their Soviet allies claimed it ran 10 miles east of the river and just east of the village of Nomonhan.

In the following spring the Japanese launched an offensive to take the Nomonhan area. The existing border bulged east of the river around the village and hill of Nomonhan and the Japanese planned to attack this 46-mile-wide and 10-mile-deep salient to test the Mongolian and Soviet armies.

The Japanese orchestrated an incident on 11 May 1939 when a few hundred Inner Mongolian Bargut horsemen, accompanied by 'advisors' from General Komatsubara's 23rd Division, crossed the border and rode to Nomonhan. Startled locals alerted the frontier guards manning a log fort on the west bank of the river some 5 miles away. On 13 May Outer Mongolian Tsirik cavalry returned and this time the Manchukuo forces were unable to budge them.

The following day the Japanese decided to reinforce them with Colonel Yaozo Azuma's 64th Regiment from the 23rd Division. The local Tsiriks were driven back and called on Major Bykov, the local Russian advisor, for help. Before he arrived, however, the Japanese Air Force flattened the log fort. Bykov, sensing that something was afoot, called for reinforcements in the form of the 6th Mongolian Cavalry Division and some Red Army detachments. Before this force could be deployed, the Japanese prudently withdrew.

On 22 May, Bykov cautiously crossed the river during the hours of darkness to assess the lie of the land. The Japanese were waiting for him and he had to conduct a fighting withdrawal back across the Khalkhin-Gol. Three days later, Bykov moved 10,000 mainly Mongolian troops over the river, cleared the eastern bank and reoccupied the village of Nomonhan. This border incident was now escalating into all-out war and on 28 May, 5,000 Japanese troops, supported by local tribesmen, attacked Bykov at daybreak. The Russians once more conducted a withdrawal back to the west bank of the river. The Mongolians then returned with Soviet support and surrounded Azuma's force. In the fighting that followed the Japanese lost 105 dead and 34 wounded. Moscow, already alert to what was happening, authorised Red Army reinforcements, and as Bykov was retreating, the 149th Motorised Infantry Regiment arrived to be thrown into the fight. Throughout the night the Japanese probed their defences but in the morning a joint Soviet-Mongolian counter-attack drove the Japanese back to the border yet again.

On 2 June 1939 Corps Commander, Georgi Konstantinovich Zhukov, was summoned to Moscow to see the People's Commissar of Defence, Marshal Klementi E. Voroshilov, who briefed him on the situation in the Far East: 'Japanese troops have made a surprise attack and crossed into friendly Mongolia which the Soviet Government is committed to defend from external aggression by the Treaty of 12 March 1936. Here is a map of the invasion area showing the situation as of 30 May.' Afterwards Zhukov went to see Ivan Smorodinov, Acting Deputy Chief of the General Staff, who told him, 'pull no punches'.

On 5 June Zhukov arrived at 57th Special Corps HQ at Tamtsak-Bulak in Mongolia and met Corps Commander N.V. Feklenko, Regimental Commissar M.S. Nikishev (who was Corps Commissar) and Brigade Commander A.M. Kushchev, Chief of Staff. To his irritation the situation was a mess; the HQ had little appreciation of the situation, communication was non-existent and coordination lacking.

Zhukov was displeased to find that none of the commanders except for Nikishev had even visited the front and therefore had little idea of what was happening. Grasping the situation, he travelled up to the front and found that local intelligence was poor. Zhukov quickly came to the assessment that 57th Corps in its present state was not up to the job of stopping the Japanese.

Zhukov immediately sent his report to Moscow, stating that he planned that the Soviet-Mongolian troops should maintain the bridgehead on the right bank of the Khalkhin-Gol, while preparing for a counter-offensive against the Japanese. Voroshilov agreed and the ineffectual Feklenko found himself replaced by Zhukov. The latter's first move was to request reinforcements for the air force, plus three rifle divisions, a tank brigade and artillery.

However, the local appraisal did confirm that the Japanese build-up signalled something more serious than a border raid was afoot. The activities of the Japanese Air Force indicated that something major was brewing. Indeed the Japanese were preparing for Operation 'Second Period of the Nomonhan Incident', which was intended to surround and rout the Soviet-Mongolian forces east of the Khalkhin-Gol, then strike across the river and destroy all Soviet-Mongolian reserves. What the Japanese did not know was that Zhukov was about to give them a major lesson in tank warfare which would secure the Soviet Union's eastern frontier until 1945.

Camouflaged Soviet T-26 light tanks photographed in 1938. As a prelude to Khalkhin-Gol, the Soviets and Japanese fought at Lake Khasan in July 1938. When the Japanese demanded the withdrawal of Soviet troops from the disputed Changkufeng Hill west of the lake, fighting broke out involving armour on both sides. The Soviet 2nd Mechanised Brigade, the 32nd and the 40th Independent Tank Battalions deployed 257 T-26s, of which 76 tanks were damaged and 9 burned.

A Red Army counter-attack ensured that the Japanese were driven back during the brief battle at Lake Khasan.

The rather formidable-looking Japanese Type 89B *I-Go Otsu* medium tank. In Manchuria it was supplemented by the Type 95 *Ha-Go* light tank and the brand new Type 97 *Chi-Ha* medium tank. The Japanese 3rd Tank Regiment had 26 Type 89s during the Nomonhan Incident – better known as the Battle of Khalkhin-Gol.

The Japanese 3rd and 4th Tank regiments deployed the Type 94 (seen below) and Type 97 tankettes against the Red Army during the fighting in Mongolia in 1939. These were ill-equipped to cope with the Soviet anti-tank guns and 45mm high-velocity guns of the Soviet BT-5 and BT-7 light tanks.

Japanese troops with captured Soviet equipment.

During the 1930s the Japanese Army's principal anti-tank gun was the Type 94 37mm which proved effective against light Soviet armour. Once in position this was awkward to manoeuvre as the embedded spades on the trails hampered rapid traverse.

Mongolian machine-gunners with a Soviet DP 28 light machine-gun.

Mongolian cavalry mounted on tiny ponies. These hardy fighters were ideal for reconnaissance on the Mongolian steppe, and kept a close watch on Japanese movements.

Japanese Type 95 *Ha-Go* tanks captured by the Red Army at Khalkhin-Gol in 1939. Some Type 95s deployed in Manchuria had their suspensions modified to counter violent pitching caused by the difficult local terrain – these were dubbed the Type 35 (Special).

A Soviet T-26 races across open ground during the battle for Mount Bain-Tsagen. Zhukov's armour was exposed over an area of 250 square miles. The fighting in Manchuria revealed a weakness in this tank's riveted armour.

Mongolian leader Khorloogiin Choibalsan, flanked by Georgi Zhukov on the right and Grigori Shtern on the left. Zhukov galvanised the Red Army into launching a highly effective armoured counter-attack against the Japanese at Khalkhin-Gol.

A Red Army BA-6/10 armoured car. Zhukov massed 346 armoured cars and 498 tanks for his counter-offensive. His Blitzkrieg was a foretaste of things to come during the Second World War.

Chapter Four

Khalkhin-Gol

By July 1939 the Japanese had massed some 38,000 men, supported by 135 tanks and 225 aircraft, east of the Khalkhin-Gol River. The outnumbered Zhukov could muster little more than 12,500 Soviet-Mongolian troops, though his main asset was a force of 186 tanks and 226 armoured cars. Notably the Soviet armour comprised the T-26 light tank as well as the BT-5 and BT-7 fast tanks. The Japanese relied on the Type 97 – which although a match for the BT tanks, were too few in number – and the slower Type 89 medium tanks.

Zhukov and his men soon found to their alarm that the BT-5 and BT-7 tanks were highly flammable, especially as they had numerous apertures through which Japanese Molotov cocktails could penetrate. Hasty field modifications included wire nets and the use of diesel fuel. Fortunately for them, superior speed and range partly compensated for the defects.

In the meantime General Komatsubara was authorised to expel the invaders in a two-pronged attack. The Japanese planned to launch a tank-led general assault along the front, while another force swung round the Soviet left flank over the river and onto the high ground of Mount Bain-Tsagen, which dominates the west bank of the river. This assault would then strike south, cutting the Soviets off. They hoped to achieve all this before the autumn rains made movement difficult.

Four regiments from the Japanese 23rd Division were tasked to cross the Khalkhin-Gol, take Bain-Tsagen and then secure the Kawatama Bridge. The second prong, under Major-General Yasuoka Masaomi with four infantry/artillery regiments and two armoured regiments, was to attack the Soviet troops on the east bank and north of the Holsten River. The Japanese struck on 2 July and their tanks and infantry soon reached the river. Zhukov decided to bide his time before showing his hand. The following day the Japanese threw a pontoon bridge over the river near Bain-Tsagen.

The Japanese pushed 10,000 troops, 100 pieces of artillery and 60 anti-tank guns onto the mountain. The defenders from the Mongolian 6th Cavalry Division could muster barely 1,000 men and 50 guns, including those on the eastern bank of the river. The Japanese seized Mount Bain-Tsagen and advanced south along the west bank. Colonel I.M. Afonin, Senior Soviet Advisor to the Mongolian Army, arrived to find that the Japanese had driven the Mongolians onto the north-western part of the mountain. He quickly appraised 57th Corps of the situation.

Zhukov, alert to the danger of his forces on the east bank being cut off, ordered a three-pronged counter-attack with 450 tanks and armoured cars. At his command he had the 11th Tank Brigade equipped with 150 tanks, the 7th Armoured Brigade with another 154 armoured vehicles and the Mongolian 8th Armoured Battalion armed with 45mm guns.

The 11th Tank Brigade under Commander Yakolev was instructed to strike from the north, supported by the 24th Motorised Regiment, which pressed in from the north-west supported by artillery under Colonel Fedyuinsky. In addition, the 7th Armoured Brigade under Colonel Lesovoi was to attack from the south supported by an armoured battalion from the Mongolian 8th Cavalry Division. Heavy guns were moved up from the 185th Artillery Regiment to support the attack on Bain-Tsagen and the 9th Armoured Brigade on the Khalkhin-Gol bridgehead.

Zhukov noted with satisfaction:

Thus, our trump card was the armour, which we decided to send into action immediately in order to crush the Japanese troops which had just crossed the river, not letting them dig in and organise anti-tank defences. There was no time to lose, since the enemy, who saw our tanks advance, rapidly began to take defensive measures and started bombing them. The tanks had no shelter. For hundreds of kilometres around us the terrain was absolutely open. There was not even a bush in sight.

At 07:00hrs on 3 July the Soviet Air Force and artillery commenced softening-up the Japanese positions. At 09:00hrs the tanks of the 11th Tank Brigade moved up with the full attack being launched at 10:45hrs. Japanese defences and anti-tank guns proved inadequate and the Russians began to make ground.

The Japanese were taken completely by surprise. Nakamura, a Japanese soldier, in his captured diary revealed:

Several scores of tanks attacked unexpectedly, causing chaos amongst our troops. There was terrible confusion. Horses stampeded, neighing and dragging gun carriages with them: cars scattered in all directions. Two of our planes were shot down. The morale of our troops fell. Japanese soldiers could be heard using such words as 'terrible', 'sad', 'dispirited', 'ghastly', etc more and more often.

The Japanese response was to launch a counter-attack on 4 July, but it came to grief in the face of Russian bombers and artillery. The bombers also successfully severed the pontoon bridge. That night General Komatsubara gave the order to withdraw and the Japanese were thrown back over the river by 5 July, though their engineers blew up the remaining bridges to prevent the Soviet tanks following, leaving many Japanese soldiers with little option but to swim for it. Those troops remaining on the eastern slopes of Bain-Tsagen were annihilated. Although Komatsubara and his HQ got back across the river, hundreds of his men drowned. He left much of his 10,000-strong force behind, strewn over the mountain.

'Thousands of dead bodies, carcasses of horses, a multitude of crashed and broken guns, mortars, machine guns and cars littered Bain-Tsagen mountain,' recalled Zhukov. The Yasuoka detachment attacked on the night of 5 July, losing over half its armour and failed to reach the Kawatama Bridge. They were counter-attacked on 9 July and driven back and Major-General Yasuoka found himself relieved of his duties. An even bigger blow for the Japanese was the loss of half the available tanks in Manchuria. The Soviets also brought down 45 Japanese aircraft, including 20 dive-bombers.

A column of Japanese Type 89 tanks rumbled across the Mongolian plain on 21 July in a show of strength, which actually did nothing but show how vulnerable they were to Soviet artillery and air attack. The Japanese tried again on 23, launching the 64th and 72nd Divisions at the Soviet forces holding the Kawatama Bridge. They used up half their ammunition stocks in a two-day preliminary barrage. The Soviets, though, held their ground, and on 25 July the Japanese, having suffered over 5,000 casualties, gave up. Between 23 July and 4 August the Japanese Air Force, according to Soviet sources, also lost 116 aircraft. The Japanese counter-attacked on 12 August, driving the Mongolian 22nd Cavalry Regiment from the Bolshie Peski height to the south.

At this point it would have been prudent for the Kwantung to call it a day and call in the diplomats, but instead more anti-tank gun units were summoned ready for a counter-attack. During early August the 75,000-strong Japanese 6th Army, under General Ogisu Rippo, was bolstered by the 7th and 23rd Infantry Divisions, a Manchukuo brigade and three cavalry regiments supported by 182 tanks, 300 armoured cars, three artillery regiments and 450 aircraft. They planned to attack along a 43-mile front on 24 August, however Zhukov was to beat them to it by four days.

Zhukov's Soviet-Mongolian command prepared for a knockout counter-offensive. Reinforcements were brought up including two rifle divisions, a tank brigade and two artillery regiments, as well as supporting bomber and fighter units. Stalin, conscious that Nazi Germany would be closely watching events in Central Asia, despatched further reinforcements. These included three infantry and two cavalry divisions, seven independent brigades (including five armoured), additional artillery and air force units to create the First Army Group.

While the Japanese had a railhead within a few miles of the border, the nearest Russian one was 403 miles away. Zhukov did not allow this or Mongolia's roads to impede his plans. Every available vehicle, including artillery tractors, was pressed into service and he amassed 55,000 tons of supplies including 18,000 tons of artillery ammunition, 6,500 tons of aircraft ammunition and 15,000 tons of fuel.

Zhukov also ensured that his deception measures lulled the Japanese into a false sense of security. He made it appear that his forces were simply strengthening their defences and hid his armour under camouflage and masked the sound of their movements. The Japanese were completely unaware of the Soviet-Mongolian build up; many officers were so content that nothing was about to happen that they went on leave. He knew that the Japanese's greatest weakness was their lack of mobility, effective tank units and motorised infantry. This meant they would not be able to respond quickly to any Soviet attack or breakthrough.

Zhukov's armoured fist consisted of the 4th, 6th and 11th Tank Brigades and the 7th and 8th Mechanised Brigades. He was ready four days before his opponents and sought to encircle them using his North, South and Central Groups, with his armour on the wings. The Soviets deployed 50,000 troops to defend the east bank of Khalkhin-Gol and then Zhukov prepared to cross on 20 August with three rifle divisions and his armoured forces.

Waiting at their jump-off points were 35 infantry battalions supported by a mobile force of 20 cavalry squadrons, 498 tanks, 346 armoured cars and 502 guns. At 05:45hrs on 20 August, 350 Russian aircraft blasted the Japanese forward positions followed by a three-hour artillery and mortar bombardment.

A Japanese conscript by the name of Fakuta recalled: 'Thousands of shells are falling close to us. It is frightening. The observation posts are doing everything possible to spot the enemy artillery, but without success because enemy bombers bomb and fighters strafe our troops. The enemy is triumphant all along the front.'

At 08:45hrs Zhukov's tanks roared forward to overwhelm the remaining Japanese – or at least so they thought. One Russian division from the Urals, the 82nd Rifle Division, was thrown back and then pinned down. Both the divisional commander and chief of staff were relieved of their duties; Zhukov sent one of his own officers and the attack was renewed.

By the next day, to the south Russian forces had swung behind the Japanese reaching the Khalkhin-Gol's east–west tributary, the Khailastyn-Gol. On 23 August the Northern Group supported by Zhukov's reserves, the 212th Airborne Brigade, fighting as infantry, seized the Palet Heights and swung south. Although trapped, the Japanese resisted to the last and the Russians lost 600 men clearing the heights.

The two wings of Zhukov's attack linked up at Nomonhan on 25 August, trapping the Japanese 23rd Division. The following day Japanese forces outside the pocket tried to get through to them, but were met by the Soviet 6th Tank Brigade. Having trapped the Japanese, Zhukov spent a week eradicating the survivors. To get at those ensconced on the Remizov Heights, his engineers assisted his tanks over the Khailastyn-Gol by reinforcing the riverbed and by 31 August it was all over.

Zhukov's successful campaign at Khalkhin-Gol severely mauled the Kwantung. The Japanese claimed they lost 8,440 dead and suffered 8,766 wounded, while the Russians claimed 9,284 casualties; however losses for the Japanese have been put as high as 45,000 killed and Russian casualties at well over 17,000. Certainly of the 60,000 Japanese troops trapped in Zhukov's cauldron, 50,000 were listed as killed, wounded and missing. In particular the Japanese 23rd Division lost 99 per cent of its strength. While Zhukov gained invaluable experience of tank warfare that was to stand him in good stead for defending Moscow from the Nazis, the Japanese singularly failed to benefit in any way from it.

A Soviet BT tank crossing the Khalkhin-Gol River. These tanks were armed with a 45mm gun with a muzzle velocity of 2,000ft per second, which meant they could penetrate Japanese tanks at over 1,000m. In contrast the Type 95 only had an effective range of less than 700m.

Soviet armour massing at Khalkhin-Gol ready for the counter-attack. These Red Army infantry are following a BT-7 light tank.

The commander and officers of the Soviet 149th Rifle Regiment just before Zhukov's counter-offensive. Note the supporting BT tanks in the background.

The Soviet BT-5 fast tank went into production in 1932 and saw combat at Khalkhin-Gol. Some 498 BT-5 and BT-7 tanks were committed to the battle. The Japanese had a low opinion of these petrol-powered tanks as they were vulnerable to Molotov cocktails.

At Khalkhin-Gol the Japanese 1st Tank Corps 3rd Tank Regiment was equipped with 26 Type 89 medium tanks, while the 4th Tank Regiment had 35 Type 95 light tanks (seen below), just eight Type 89s and three Type 94 tankettes. The 37mm gun on the Japanese Type 95 light tank, despite its mediocre performance, was effective against the T-26.

A knocked-out Type 89 which was essentially a copy of the British Vickers Medium C; the Japanese had too few of these. Likewise the 3rd Tank Regiment was supplemented with just four new Type 97 *Chi-Ha* medium tanks. One of these was used as a commander's tank and, after getting entangled in barbed wire, was destroyed by BT-7 tanks and anti-tank guns.

The Japanese Type 97 *Te-Ke* light tank's first taste of real combat came during the fighting in Mongolia against the Red Army. Assigned to the Japanese infantry divisions, they went up against the high-velocity 45mm guns of the Soviet BT-5 and BT-7 light tanks. The *Te-Ke* appeared in a number of variants, including self-propelled gun, ammunition carrier, observation vehicle and balloon mooring.

The obsolete Japanese Type 38 75mm field gun dated from the early 1900s but still saw service during the Second Sino-Japanese War, the Soviet-Japanese border wars and the war in the Pacific.

Japanese infantry gathered in front of knocked-out Soviet BA-10 armoured cars.

A Japanese Type 94/92 tankette (based on the British Carden-Loyd MK VI), captured by the Red Army in Mongolia.

Russian troops examine an intact Japanese Type 95 *Ha-Go* light tank also captured in Mongolia (this appears to be the same vehicle shown on p. 45).

Japanese prisoners taken by Zhukov at Khalkhin-Gol. The Imperial Japanese Army lost around 50,000 men in the face of the Red Army's successful counter-offensive.

Chapter Five

When Tigers Fight: The Sequel

After the Nomonhan Incident, the shortcomings of the Type 94 37mm anti-tank gun had become obvious, and the Imperial Japanese Army started the development of a new anti-tank weapon that could be more effective against the new Soviet tanks. However, given that a new design would take time to produce, as an interim measure the existing Type 94 gun was modified with a longer barrel to provide greater armour penetration. Designated the Type 1 37mm anti-tank gun, it was issued to combat units in 1941. This was just in time for a renewal of hostilities with the Chinese.

On paper, China had 3.8 million men under arms organised into 246 'frontline' divisions, with another 70 divisions assigned to protect rear areas by 1941. As many as 40 Chinese infantry divisions were equipped with European-manufactured weapons and were trained by foreign (particularly German and Soviet) instructors. The rest were understrength and generally untrained units of indifferent quality. While the NRA impressed many Western military observers, they felt it more like a nineteenth-century rather than a twentieth-century army in terms of training and outlook. In reality it remained firmly rooted as an infantry force lacking tanks and mechanisation.

The Japanese were inevitably greatly helped by tensions between China's Nationalist and Communist forces that had been at each other's throats in the mid-1930s. While some of Mao's Communist units had escaped north on the Long March to Shaanxi, others remained in central China. In early 1941 fresh fighting between the NRA and the Communists only served to undermine China's defences.

By the end of 1940 the Chinese Communist New 4th Army was occupying a vast area of Jiangsu and Anhui in central China, with some 35,000 men under arms. Chen Yi, later to succeed Zhou Enlai as Mao's Foreign Minister, was one of the divisional commanders who played a deadly game of cat-and-mouse by harassing the Japanese at every turn. When this army was ordered north of the Yellow River it ended up fighting the NRA's 40th Division. This broke the uneasy alliance against Japan, fatally weakening the Chinese war effort.

Despite this, the campaigns of 1941 did not substantially advance Japan's strategic position in a country it found easy to invade but impossible to conquer. Japanese forces broke through Chinese defences in southern Henan at Chantaiguan and at Minggang in January 1941. They also conducted operations in northern Jiangxi at Fancheng, where they were rebuffed, and also near Nanchang. Then, on 7 December 1941, Japan took the pressure off China by bombing the US fleet at anchor in Pearl Harbor and invaded the British base of Hong Kong. It also meant that China became a recipient of US Lend-Lease material, including much-needed M3 and M4 tanks.

After its experiences with tanks at Khalkhin-Gol, Shanghai and Nanking, the Imperial Japanese Army did not abandon concerted mechanised warfare entirely. The Japanese military belatedly came to the conclusion by mid-1942 that they should concentrate their armoured regiments deployed in Manchuria into divisions.

The Japanese 1st Tank Brigade was created on 24 June 1942 out of four separate armoured regiments based in Manchukuo. With the addition of one infantry regiment, it was soon raised to the status of a full armoured division. This unit was stationed in Ning'an in northern Manchukuo. The 2nd Tank Division was also raised in Manchukuo at the same time as was the 3rd Tank Division in Mengjiang as part of the Japanese Northern China Area Army under the overall responsibility of the Mongolia Garrison Army.

At this stage the main priority for the Japanese in China was to crush the Chinese government and the NRA by invading its last stronghold – Sichuan province. However, the necessary resources could not be brought to bear for such a massive undertaking after the Japanese naval defeat at Midway and the American landings on Guadalcanal. Plans for massing 16 divisions in south-central China brought in from the Japanese mainland, Manchuria and the South Seas to reinforce the Japanese Expeditionary Force had to be quickly abandoned. The Chinese took the opportunity to reorganise their forces. Meanwhile, General Stillwell, commanding Nationalist troops in support of the British Army, prepared for a Chinese counter-attack in Burma.

For its final grand offensive of the war launched in May 1944, the Japanese massed 400–500 tanks and other armoured fighting vehicles in southern Henan. The aim of Operation Ichi-Go was to destroy the main enemy airbases in south-west China from where American bombers were attacking Japanese targets with devastating effect. The Japanese also wanted to secure the lines of communication between their armies in central and northern China. This was the first genuinely large-scale strategic offensive undertaken by the Japanese in China since 1938.

Operation Ichi-Go was divided into two parts; in the northern sector Operation

Kogo along the Beijing–Wuhan railway (mainly in Henan province), and Operation Togo in the southern sector centred on Hunan. From Wuhan the Japanese forces also struck southward along the railway line as far as the Vietnamese border. The Japanese took advantage of the flat Henan plain to deploy their tanks on a large scale. Other Japanese forces moved northwards along the railway line from Xinyang in south Henan.

Operation Kogo was conducted against 390,000 Chinese troops under General Tang Enbo, holding the strategic position before Luoyang. In late April the Japanese 12th Army, spearheaded by the 3rd Tank Division, crossed the Yellow River around Zhengzhou and defeated Enbo's forces near Xuchang. It then swung clockwise to besieged Luoyang, defended by three Chinese divisions.

The 3rd Tank Division led the assault on Luoyang on 13 May which was taken on 25 May. The division's 8th Armoured Regiment (formerly based in Mukden) was redeployed in June 1944 to support the Japanese 8th Area Army in Rabaul in the Pacific.

They captured Lingbao at the westernmost tip of Henan province on 11 June 1944. By this stage the Japanese lines of communication were stretched and the mountains hampered their tanks, but the entire length of the strategic railway was in Japanese hands despite the efforts of the Chinese Army. In addition, by November the US Air Force had lost 7 of its 12 Chinese airbases, forcing the Americans to island-hop ever closer to mainland Japan.

Chinese soldiers of the National Revolutionary Army wearing British-supplied helmets and operating a Czech-supplied ZB vz. 26 light machine-gun.

Chinese troops in 1939, again wearing British Army helmets.

A Chinese NRA soldier wearing a very distinctive German-supplied M35 helmet.

Following the Japanese attack on Pearl Harbor, the Chinese Nationalist leader, Generalissimo Chiang Kai-Shek allied himself with the British and Americans. This ensured him military supplies from America including much-needed tanks.

A Chinese NRA M5 light tank preserved as a war memorial.

Chinese troops with American-supplied Stuart light tanks which formed Chiang's new armoured forces.

擦照燈
砲塔蓋
砲眼
砲塔
銃眼
車体
前部出入口扉
牽環
履帯
起動輪
下部転輪
ばね覆
揺臂
上部転輪
誘導輪

拳銃口
展望窓
消音器
後部出入口扉
後部牽環

The Japanese Type 95 *Ha-Go* gave the Japanese a distinct advantage over the Chinese armies that comprised largely infantry.

A Type 97 *Chi-Ha* radio operator. This tank was introduced in 1938 and saw action against the American, British, Chinese and Soviet Armies.

The Japanese Type 11 infantry gun was operated by a five- to ten-man squad, though in action only really required two gunners.

The Japanese Model 96 (1936) 150mm howitzer was one of the Imperial Japanese Army's largest artillery pieces. It continued to be used as the main howitzer of Japanese artillery units until the end of the Second World War.

The Type 1 47mm gun was introduced in 1941/42 to supplement the Japanese Type 94 and Type 1 37mm anti-tank guns.

Chinese troops wearing the German M35 helmet are seen here passing out in 1944.

Chapter Six

Fortress Singapore

The Battle of Khalkhin-Gol convinced the Japanese to strike south into South-East Asia against British, French and Dutch interests and south into the Pacific against the Americans at Pearl Harbor. Japan reasoned that with the Western Allies distracted by their war against Hitler, they would not have sufficient resources to counter Japanese ambitions toward their colonial possessions. These contained key natural resources, including oil and rubber, all of which was needed by the Japanese war machine.

The Japanese proceeded to wage aerial, land and naval war on a truly grand scale that made the fighting in Manchuria and China pale into insignificance. Japanese armies passed through French Indochina (Vietnam and Laos) with the acquiescence of the Vichy government and neutral Siam (Thailand) to attack the weak British military garrisons in Burma and Malaya. At the same time Japanese task forces departed from Formosa to strike the American bases in the Philippines – most notably Luzon Island.

The Japanese Navy attacked the US Fleet at Pearl Harbor on 7 December 1941. The very next day Japanese troops began to land in Thailand and Malaya as well as attacking the mainland defences of the British colony at Hong Kong. British III Corps headquartered in Kuala Lumpur had its work cut out trying to defend Malaya's vast coastline. To the north, defending the border with Thailand, was the 11th Indian Division between Jitra and Kroh, while to the east 9th Indian Division was in the Kuala Krai area.

During the 1930s conventional British military thinking was that the dense jungles and rubber plantations of Malaya were not at all suitable for mechanised warfare. In addition, the key choke point for vehicles heading south was about 24 miles into Thailand north of the Malaya/Thai border. Known as 'The Ledge', this was a stretch of road carved along the edge of a steep hill; if it fell into Japanese hands it would allow them to invade Malaya via the interior road. If this happened it would compromise the main British position in north-western Malaya at Jitra by opening the flank. Likewise British defensive plans also hung on being able to cut the railway line between the Thai port of Singora and Jitra.

One of the finest moments for Japan's armour was the capture of Singapore in 1942. The invading Japanese 25th Army had a tank corps with three regiments totalling 228 medium and light tanks, which were reinforced by scout regiments assigned to three combat divisions fielding 37 light tanks. The Japanese invasion of Malaya was both high- and low-tech with Japanese forces employing artillery, bombers, fighters, tanks and bicycles.

Although the British mindset at the time was that Malaya was unsuitable for tanks, ironically Britain did consider sending light armour, as it was felt the best way to stop a tank was with another tank. General Arthur Percival commanding in Malaya asked for two regiments; medium tanks were thought to be too heavy for many of Malaya's bridges, so some consideration was given to sending light tanks which would be manned by Australian crews. Tanks, though, were not available before war broke out. In the meantime Malaya Command was not blind to the threat posed by enemy armour and issued orders in April 1941 stating: 'All officers must be tank-minded. Against an enemy equipped with tanks movement must be from anti-tank obstacle to anti-tank obstacle.' Nevertheless there is no evidence to suggest that combined arms anti-tank exercises were conducted in Malaya and available War Office pamphlets on tank fighting were not issued to the garrison.

To make matters worse, most British Imperial forces were not equipped or trained to cope with jungle warfare. The Indian brigades sent as reinforcements in 1941 had trained to fight in the Middle East and had, broadly speaking, never seen a tank. All the Australian and Indian units sent to Malaya travelled light for the sake of speed. The issuing of weapons such as light machine-guns and field artillery was critically slow when they arrived. In the event the British Army had to rely on about three dozen armoured cars and open-topped carriers (Universal or Bren – neither of which were suitable for armoured warfare – though 2-pounder anti-tank guns and mines were available). The Japanese Type 97 tank would not have coped with the 2-pounder gun or the armour of the British Matilda or Valentine tanks, but none of these were sent.

Alistair Urquhart, serving with the Gordon Highlanders, was stationed at Fort Canning, the British military HQ on Singapore. In his memoirs *The Forgotten Highlander*, Urquhart recalled how the British Army got it so badly wrong.

> Japanese troops under General Yamashita, who would later become known as 'The Tiger of Malaya', were storming south at an unbelievable speed, relying on bicycles and the ingenuity of their engineers, who quickly restored sabotaged bridges and roads. Critically the Japanese infantry were supported by three hundred tanks. The war machines that the British Army had decided were

unsuitable for conditions in Malaya cut great swathes through our lightly armed troops.

Following Japanese seaborne landings on the western coast of southern Thailand and northern Malaya at Singora, Patani and Kota Bharu, British forces did not move north until 10 hours after the invasion in a vain effort to block 'The Ledge'. Elements of the 11th Indian Division, a battalion strength battlegroup named *Krohcol*, crossed the border at 15:00hrs on 8 December 1941 and found themselves opposed by Thai police. Having only advanced just over a mile the advance guard decided to stop for the night and await the rest of the battlegroup that had been delayed.

By 10 December *Krohcol* were within 3½ miles of their destination when they came into contact with Japanese troops led by tanks. The first one was hit by an anti-tank rifle and withdrew. Now that 'The Ledge' was already in Japanese hands, there was little prospect of taking it. The following day, while Lieutenant Colonel H.D. Moorhead sought permission to retreat, the Japanese brought forward two battalions supported by at least one tank company. The Japanese attacked on 12 December, forcing the battlegroup back towards the border.

The Japanese push south on Jitra opened when a spearhead of 500 troops supported by two dozen light tanks and some light guns advanced on prepared defensive positions held by nearly 14,000 men supported by 50 field guns and 36 anti-tank guns of the 11th Indian Division. The Japanese kept their tanks at the front and used them to blast a way through or to pin down the defenders while their flanks were turned. They brushed aside the Indian and Gurkha screening forces after two battalions were caught off guard by armour on the road and scattered. The Japanese captured Jitra on 12 December followed by Gurun three days later. To the west the town of Kroh had been taken by 14 December. Japanese tanks then converged on Taiping and advanced on Ipoh.

In the early hours of 7 January 1942 a battlegroup of 30 Japanese tanks, a battalion of motorised infantry and a battery of light artillery forced their way down the road at Slim River. This was a key defensive point north of Kuala Lumpur. Two tanks were lost to mines, followed by three more to anti-tank guns and anti-tank rifles. Ultimately though, nothing the defenders could do would stop them, following a series of bad judgement calls. Breaking through, the tanks outstripped their infantry and ran amok behind British lines.

Major W.J. Winkfield leading a Gurkha battalion, recalled: 'Sudden sense of unease behind me and something grazed my leg. Looked to see a tank bearing down on me. Dived into ditch. After tanks passed found battalion had vanished except for a few casualties.' Winkfield only managed to round up a dozen men out of over 500.

Some 25-pounder guns that could have been brought to bear on the Japanese tanks were caught still hitched to their tractors as their crews ate breakfast.

Further down the road an anti-aircraft battery with 40mm guns put up a fight but they had no armour-piercing rounds and could not penetrate the tanks' frontal armour. In just over five hours the Japanese pushed through two brigades and covered over 21 miles. Only when they ran into a Royal Artillery unit equipped with 4.5-in howitzers, which blew apart the lead tank at point-blank range and damaged a second, did they stop and await reinforcements.

At Slim River just 30 Japanese tanks supported by 1,000 troops finished off two brigades. The 11th Indian Division lost 3,000 prisoners along with a month's worth of supplies, plus 50 Bren Carriers and dozens of lorries. It was not long before Japanese armour was pushing through Kuala Lumpur itself and on the road to Malacca and Singapore.

On the west coast, Japanese tanks unhinged the entire British defence. With the collapse of 11th Indian Division, the 9th Indian was at risk of being cut off. Such a situation now ruled out any prospect of counter-attack. During the retreat south from the port of Kuantan on the east coast, Eric Lomax, with the Royal Signals, feared becoming trapped: 'I knew that just ahead of us the enemy was moving with his tanks and bicycles. I had still not seen a Japanese soldier, alive or dead. That night I was lucky, and although I failed to find a truck in working order or my missing men, I also failed to meet the Japanese.'

The most famous action of the campaign occurred in mid-January 1942 on the road between Muar and Bakri. Five Japanese tanks of the Gotanda Medium Tank Company ran into two Australian anti-tank guns from the 8th Australian Division which were positioned at the side of the road at the bottom of a reverse slope. A steep cutting at this point forced the tanks to remain trapped on the road. At point-blank range all the tanks were knocked out, while three more followed and joined the firefight. The Japanese, though, soon moved to infiltrate the Australian and Indian positions, forcing a fighting withdrawal.

Lieutenant Colonel Tsuji Masanobu, Chief Operations Officer of the Japanese 25th Army recorded: 'Between 16 and 23 January a desperate fight occurred. When the Gotanda Medium Tank Company lost all its tanks, the surviving officers and men had attacked on foot, reaching the enemy artillery position and the Parit Sulong Bridge, where the last of them met a heroic death after holding up the enemy for some time…'.

Thanks to the continual destruction of bridges and causeways in Johore, Japanese engineers were hard pressed to keep up with the repairs. The Japanese tank forces, after losses around Gemas and Bakri, had to take time to regroup. This forced the Japanese infantry to march into southern Johore initially without any tank support.

In the meantime British and other Imperial troops continued to fall back to Johore Baru and then Singapore.

Japanese forces landed on Singapore Island on 8 February 1942. Nearly all their remaining tanks units were used to reinforce the Japanese 5th Division which was tasked with breaching the city's defences. It attacked along the trunk road sparking heavy fighting south of the reservoirs that supplied water to the trapped population.

Captain Reginald Burton, serving with the Royal Norfolk Regiment defending Singapore, was shocked to find the Japanese had little fear of armoured vehicles. Upon hearing that some of their men were having trouble withdrawing from the racecourse, Burton recalled:

> The CO [Commanding Officer] ordered the carrier platoon to counter-attack and rescue them. They roared into action. The carrier platoon officer was very brave, but also impetuous. We heard afterwards that he drove straight at the enemy. There was a mêlée. A Japanese officer jumped from a tree on to the carrier and severed his head with a great sweep of a samurai sword. This was perhaps our first stark indication of the Japs' barbaric lust for killing.

The Japanese 18th Division struck along the south coast of Singapore Island. Although it suffered during the first four days of fighting, it was spurred on by the thought of the 5th Division reaching Singapore first. The garrison's defences were strong along the southern Pasir Panjang Ridge, which was held by the 1st Malaya Regiment and Australian carriers. Nevertheless capture of the coastal guns and control of the air ensured Japanese victory.

Much to the humiliation of the British Army, in mid-February 1942 General Percival surrendered with the loss of 80,000 Australian, British and Indian troops who were captured. They joined another 50,000 taken during the Malayan Campaign. The Japanese victory, thanks to their tenacity, tanks and bombers, had been swift and mirrored the German Blitzkrieg in Europe.

Indian troops in Singapore in November 1941. During the war the Indian Army fought in South-East Asia, North Africa, Italy and the Middle East.

Allied troops pass a knocked-out Type 95 *Ha-Go*. This tank went into service in the mid-1930s and saw action in China and throughout the Far East.

A knocked-out *Chi-Ha* with its distinctive short-barrelled 57mm gun. The twisted cable round the turret is all that remains of the radio frame aerial. The Type 97 *Chi-Ha* medium tank was used to good effect against the British in Malaya and at Singapore. One of the main improvements of the *Chi-Ha* over earlier Japanese tanks was that the two-man turret enabled the commander to direct the tank rather than having to double-up as the gunner.

Type 95 *Ha-Go* tank destroyed in the Battle of Muar in January 1942 by an Australian 2-pounder anti-tank gun during the Malayan Campaign.

An Australian 2-pounder gun of 13th Battery, 4th Anti-Tank Regiment, firing on Japanese Type 95 *Ha-Go* tanks of the 14th Tank Regiment on the Muar–Parit Sulong road, 18 January 1942.

One of six *Ha-Go* tanks destroyed by an Australian 2-pounder gun in the Battle of Muar. The escaping crew were killed by Allied infantry covering the artillery.

Type 95 *Ha-Go* tanks belonging to the 3rd Company of the 14th Tank Regiment destroyed by Australian gunfire near Bakri during the Malayan Campaign.

An Australian 25-pounder gun crew preparing to open fire on approaching Japanese at Bakri in mid-January 1942.

Japanese troops mopping up British resistance in the Malayan capital Kuala Lumpur.

Japanese Type 89 medium tank photographed in the jungle during the operations to push the US and Filipino forces back into the Bataan Peninsula in the Philippines. Although the Type 89 was being withdrawn from frontline service by 1942, units equipped with this tank still saw combat in the Battle of the Philippines, the Battle of Malaya and the Burma Campaign. The Japanese Army also continued to use them in China.

Japanese troops celebrating their victory at Bataan, which involved the 7th Tank Regiment.

American troops surrendering at Corregidor.

Japanese Type 89s moving toward the Filipino capital Manila. In Malaya and in the Philippines, Japanese tanks swept all before them in rapid succession.

Chapter Seven

Island Hopping

The experiences of the US 1st Armored Division in North Africa quickly illustrated just how useless the M3 and M5 light tanks were against the German medium and heavy panzers. The tank's 37mm shell simply bounced off the Panzer IV and Tiger. This led to a major reduction in light tank strength and their replacement by medium tanks in the US armoured divisions. However, in the Pacific the M3 and M5 was quite often the only tank available. Both the Americans and Japanese were slow to adapt to the realities of armoured warfare in the region. This was in part because the conditions on the islands were not conducive to the deployment of tanks, where the restrictive terrain left them largely in a support role.

Like the attack down the Malayan Peninsula at Bataan, the Japanese simply drove down the roads. Leading the assault was the Japanese 65th Brigade supported by the 7th Tank Regiment. The Japanese also had unchallenged air superiority which allowed them to bomb Bataan with impunity. Although the Japanese opened their attack on 9 January 1942 it would be four months before the trapped defenders surrendered.

The M3 Stuart was the first American tank to see action against the Japanese. It equipped the US Army's 192nd and 194th Tank Battalions which were shipped to Luzon in the Philippines to form a Provisional Tank Group just 18 days before the Japanese invasion. This was established under the command of Colonel James R.N. Weaver with 108 Stuarts. The inexperienced crews who had trained on the earlier M2A2 light tank struggled to get their new M3s operational after the journey from America.

In response to the Japanese landings in the Lingayen Gulf on 22 December 1941, a small force from Weaver's Provisional Tank Group, plus other units, were sent to stem the Japanese at Damortis by holding the coast road leading south. Unfortunately just five of the Stuarts could be fuelled and sent forward in time. Meanwhile enemy tanks supported both the Japanese landings at Caba and at Agoo to the north of Damortis.

The first US tank-versus-tank combat occurred on 22 December, when a platoon of five M3s led by Lieutenant Ben R. Morin fought Type 95 *Ha-Go*s of the Japanese

4th Tank Regiment north of Damortis. While manoeuvring off the road, Lieutenant Morin's tank took a direct hit and began to burn. Morin was wounded, and he and his crew were captured. The other M3s were also hit, but managed to withdraw. The M3s of the 194th and 192nd Tank Battalions continued to skirmish with the Japanese tanks as they retreated down the Bataan Peninsula, with the last tank-versus-tank combat occurring on 7 April 1942.

Following the Japanese invasion, Forrest Knox of the 192nd Battalion was not happy at the state of affairs, saying of the ten-day withdrawal to Bataan: 'Like any other operation at the start of a war it was totally screwed up.' Inevitably the green Stuart crews soon discovered just how effective their machine-guns and 37mm anti-tank gun was against Japanese infantry. 'My buddy caught one Jap in his sights,' recalled Knox. 'He ran down the front deck and off down the trail – a 37mm at that short range was unbelievable. Hit him in the middle of the back and his arms and legs just flew off – kind of like shooting a gallon plastic jug full of water with an army rifle.'

To combat the Stuart tank, the Japanese resorted to anti-tank guns, limpet mines, Molotov cocktails and sniping at the crews. In an attempt to destroy the Stuarts, the Japanese would also clamber on board and try to prise off the filler caps so they could drop a grenade into the fuel tank. In response the tanks would shoot the Japanese troops off each other. The crews tried to prevent the grenade-in-the-fuel-tank tactic by using a 3lb hammer to bash the filler cap firmly on after refuelling.

Knox and his fellow crewmen gained on-the-job instruction on the pitfalls of the M3: 'In action we used to shut off the engine to conserve the gas. That was our shortage, not ammo. Then, without the cooling fan on the engine running, the inside quickly got like an oven. The transmission was the size of a barrel and at about 140 degrees, and the guns so hot they would cook off by themselves.'

Engaging the Japanese brought other hazards inside the tank. Knox encountered another problem with the machine-guns that clearly had not been thought through:

> The empty brass (cartridge cases) burnt a lot of men, so you had to wrap a towel around your neck and keep your collar buttoned tight to avoid burns. All pockets were cut off – [they] caught brass and held it against you. You had a choice, burn your fingers getting it out or burn your ass if you left it in.

The Japanese 7th Tank Regiment played a role in defeating the trapped American and Filipino armies in Bataan, in particular the capture of the strategically important Mount Samat, which sat in the middle of their defences. The Japanese, under Lieutenant General Masaharu Homma, assumed that 25,000 men held Bataan, though in reality there were three times as many. During January 1942 forcing the

Americans from their first line of resistance anchored on Mauban and Abucay, the Japanese suffered heavy casualties. The attackers paused while they conducted operations elsewhere. However, the defenders were left besieged, hungry and disease-ridden in the face of Japanese superiority in air power, tanks and artillery.

On 3 April 1942 the newly arrived Japanese 4th Division, supported by the tanks of Akira Nara's 65th Brigade, launched the delayed Japanese offensive to finally secure Bataan. The latter unit, comprising three infantry regiments, included the 7th Tank Regiment, as well as attached field and mountain artillery. Elements of the 21st Division, which had arrived in late February, covered the Japanese eastern flank, while the 16th Division made a feint attack to the west.

At about 09:00hrs the Japanese barrage began with almost 150 guns opening the biggest bombardment of the campaign. The Americans responded as best they could but fired blind in the face of Japanese command of the sky. The American I Corps on the right had around 50 artillery pieces, mainly of 75mm. On the left II Corps was supported by 100 guns, again mainly of 75mm, but with 31 naval guns up to 3in calibre and 12 mountain guns. The Japanese artillery and aerial bombardment lasted until the afternoon and then the ground assault began. Nara's tanks pierced the line on the flank of II Corps and pushed southwards crossing the Tiawar River where the Filipino defenders broke after brief resistance. Facing the 65th Brigade, the Filipino 41st Division ceased to exist and the neighbouring 21st Division fell back in disorder.

On 4 April Homma, a normally cautious general, abandoned all restraint and ordered his men to take Mount Samat. Nara's troops cut round the flank of the remaining defenders in his sector forcing them to retreat. A Japanese armoured thrust also gained control of the east–west Pilar–Bagac Road. By the night of 7 April the Japanese, having reached Limay on the east coast, had almost won an offensive they anticipated would last a month. Two days later they had reached Cabcaben on the southern tip of Bataan, forcing an American surrender.

Following the fall of the Philippines the Japanese used captured Stuarts for garrison duty and then against the Americans in the fighting for the Philippines in early 1945. Somewhat ironically they were the first and very last M3s to see combat in the Pacific.

While Japanese armour helped secure victory in Burma, Malaya, the Philippines and Singapore, things did not go so smoothly in the fetid jungles of New Guinea north of Australia. A combination of unfavourable terrain and unexpectedly tough opposition from Australian and American troops ensured that Japanese strategies to capture Port Moresby did not go according to plan. Japanese troops were to suffer defeat at the hands of Australian tanks at Buna.

While Australian units had been helping British and Commonwealth forces against the Germans and Italians in North Africa, Japan's entry into the war brought the threat much closer to home. Initially Australian units had no armour and very few anti-tank weapons to fend off Japanese tanks, though what they had were used to some effect in Malaya. On 23 January 1942 the Japanese overwhelmed the Australian garrison at Rabaul on the northern tip of New Britain. Then, the following month on 19 February, the Japanese bombed Australia's naval base and airbase at Darwin, sparking an invasion scare. After the landings on northern New Guinea, the Japanese tried to fight their way south over the Owen Stanley Range and down the Kokoda track from Buna.

In the meantime, landings in Milne Bay in August were intended to seize Port Moresby from the east. In their second thrust, made at night, the Japanese were supported by tanks using their headlights to dazzle and light up the terrain. Initially the Australian thought the lights were one of their own Bren Carriers, but actually belonged to two enemy tanks. Lacking anti-tank weapons, the Australians suffered heavy casualties. Attempts to bring up an anti-tank gun failed after its tow truck became bogged down and was abandoned to the Japanese.

However, the Japanese suffered heavier losses, as they did not move their tanks forward until their infantry had secured the ground. Also the tanks had to take it in turns to fight as they had to withdraw every time ammunition supplies became low. In the end, Corporal O'Brien using a Boyes anti-tank rifle, managed to destroy both.

The victors of Milne Bay were then moved east of the Japanese stronghold at Buna. They took with them four M3 Stuart tanks, but these could only operate on cleared firm ground. The peculiar terrain of such areas as New Guinea meant size and manoeuvrability were far more important than the heavier armour and more powerful armament of the Sherman. These light tanks were of great assistance while mobile, knocking holes in Japanese emplacements and protecting the infantry. In desperation, the Japanese tried to light a fire under one tank, but the attackers were killed by another tank. In early January American and Australian forces, supported by the tanks, broke the enemy defence and captured Buna.

During the war in the Pacific the US Army committed none of its armoured divisions to this theatre of war and deployed only a third of its 70 tank battalions. Understandably the US Marine Corps employed all six of its tank battalions to the island battles. Notably the US Army only ever used its M3 medium tanks once in the Pacific. In the Battle of Tarawa, US Army units were supported by a platoon of M3A5 Lee medium tanks from the 193rd Tank Battalion. The US Marines did not employ the M3 Lees; their tank battalions made do with the M3 Stuart until early 1944 when these were replaced by M4 Shermans.

The Marine tankers of Companies A and B, 1st Tank Battalion, serving with the US Marine Corps' 1st Division, were equipped with the M3 light tank. They helped spearhead the American counter-offensive in the South Pacific with the unopposed landing on Guadalcanal on 7 August 1942. Once the tanks had landed, they were deployed to cover the eastern boundary of the beachhead. Initially little offensive action was seen by either of the two tank companies.

After Company A made an unopposed crossing of the Tenaru River on Guadalcanal, they found the vital Japanese airfield undefended. The tanks were used mainly in a defensive role and were dug-in between the airfield and the beach in a circular displacement. From these positions they could deal with any counter-attack from the sea or a paratroop landing on the airfield.

Former Sergeant Major 'Vi' Viveiros recalled:

> There were two limited offensive actions. One involved a platoon of five tanks without any coordinated support, advancing from a sector of the perimeter across a large open area of thick grass. Three tanks were quickly knocked out by an anti-tank gun concealed on the far side where the heavy jungle continued. Of the two tanks that remained, one, the platoon leader's, had taken a 37mm hit dead center on the side of the turret that decapitated him. Nine of the crews of the other three tanks were killed and three escaped to safety.

The second action occurred on 21 August 1942 when Company B became caught up in the action involving up to 1,000 Japanese troops attempting to break through the American lines at the mouth of the Ilu River. The Marines crossed the river on the right flank to envelop the Japanese from behind. Five tanks crossed the sand spit at the mouth of the river and helped in mopping up enemy resistance employing canister and machine-gun fire on enemy positions. Gruesomely Viveiros remembered: 'More enemy were crushed and mangled than shot, as evidenced by the remains of flesh entwined in the tank suspension.' During the engagement, two of the tanks were disabled – one of them by a mine – but the crews were rescued by the other tanks.

The 1st Tank Battalion was then involved in the Battle of Bloody Ridge, on 13–14 September 1942. On 13 September the tanks helped repel a Japanese attack east of the airfield. The following morning at 09:45hrs, six tanks were sent to sweep the field in front of the Marines' position to prevent the Japanese hiding in the long grass. This was accomplished without incident. The tanks were then deployed at 11:00hrs to destroy an enemy machine-gun position in a native hut on the eastern side of the grassy plain.

Meanwhile the Japanese moved German-made RA 37mm anti-tank guns to the edge of a wood on the eastern side of the airfield. Once the tanks were within 50yd of the hut, using armour-piercing and high-explosive shells the Japanese knocked out three tanks in quick succession. The crews of two were rescued but the third toppled into a stream, trapping the occupants. The latter was later salvaged but the others were written off, having been smashed by the armour-piercing shells. The 1st Tank Battalion went on to take part in the bloody operations in New Guinea, New Britain, Peleliu and Okinawa.

Stuarts served with the US Marines during the liberation of New Georgia in the Solomon Islands and the clearing of the Dragon Peninsula. At Zanana a Japanese tank killer unit attempted to disable the tanks using flame-throwers and magnetic mines. It became evident that the Marine tanks were most effective in spearheading their attacks because they were relatively impervious to small arms fire and had weapons that could deal immediately with the numerous and well-hidden enemy bunkers. The tanks, though, needed to be protected at close quarters to prevent the Japanese from reaching them and attaching anti-tank mines.

On 26 and 27 July 1943, during the Battle for Bartley Ridge, six Marine tanks led the assault. These were deployed in two lines of three each with 18 infantry men armed with flame-throwers, automatic weapons, rifles and grenades providing escort. The ferocity of the Japanese fire quickly drove off the infantry and a magnetic mine was used to destroy one tank. The remaining vehicles fought from within the encircling Japanese defensive positions for five hours before withdrawing. A second tank had to be abandoned after it got stuck, while a third lost its way and was destroyed. In the end, American artillery had to be used to silence the determined Japanese defences.

M3A1 light tanks of the Marines' 3rd Tank Battalion fought at Bougainville in November 1943; the battalion also participated in the battles of Guam and Iwo Jima. The 4th Tank Battalion of the 4th Marine Division was equipped with the M5A1s when they were involved in the battles of Kwajalein 1–2 February 1944, Saipan 15 June–9 July 1944 and Tinian 24 July–1 August 1944. The M5A1 was capable of combating Japanese light and medium tanks and provided welcome support both in the gun tank role and when fitted with other weaponry.

In January 1944 the US 5th Amphibious Corps shipped 20 Ronson M3 flame-throwers to the Pacific. The Canadian Ronson flame-thrower had been intended for the Universal Carrier. After trials, it was decided to mount the weapon in a medium tank, but few were available and as the M3 light tank was being replaced by the M5 light tank it was decided to use the M3 and M3A1 instead. The Ronson replaced the 37mm gun and was protected by a howitzer-like shroud and had a traverse of 180 degrees. Four specially built fuel tanks were added that had a total capacity of 175 gallons, giving two minutes of sustained fire. Produced in Hawaii, this system was aptly dubbed the 'Satan Flame Gun'.

A Type 97 (Improved) *Shinhoto Chi-Ha* tank armed with the distinctive high-velocity 47mm gun. From 1942 onwards this became the main Japanese medium tank.

The Satan's role was to clear enemy bunkers, buildings, caves, canefields and dugouts. The 2nd and 4th Marine Divisions were issued with 12 of these flame-throwers when they landed on Saipan on 17 June 1944 (D+2). Four flame tanks and one light tank formed a platoon normally assigned to a medium tank company. They were employed continuously until 13 July and 11 days later were shipped to Tinian and were deployed with the assault wave. After the Tinian landing, 400 burned bodies were counted on the beach. Due to the vulnerability of the light tank to Japanese artillery and anti-tank guns, it was decided that medium tanks would be used in future flame-throwing roles, thus ending the Stuart's flame-throwing career.

Stuart light tanks supporting Australian troops at Buna during the New Guinea Campaign, which was fought from January 1942 to August 1945. Conditions there were far from ideal for armoured warfare.

A disabled Sherman on the shoreline of Betio, Tarawa Atoll, Gilbert Islands, which the US Marines assaulted on 20 November 1943. For some reason the tank's turret is facing rearward.

Men of the US 2nd Marine Division storming a Japanese strongpoint on Betio. The Japanese defences were well prepared and included many heavy calibre weapon positions, including 140mm and 200mm guns, both of which were deadly to tanks.

An abandoned Sherman in the Tarawa Lagoon.

A Type 95 light tank on the beach at Tarawa. The garrison were supported by 14 Type 95s.

Japanese prisoners of war. After 76 hours of fighting on Tarawa, 4,690 defenders lay dead and only 17 Japanese surrendered; a further 129 Korean labourers were also captured.

A Type 97 *Te-Ke* tankette on Namur Island, Kwajalein Atoll, which was captured in early 1944. As well as directing the tank, the commander also had to operate the turret-mounted 37mm gun or a 7.7mm machine-gun. American Shermans are just visible in the top left of the image.

Dubbed 'Lucky Legs II' by its crew, this Sherman is supporting US troops on Bougainville in March 1944. The island was assaulted on 1 November 1943, but the Japanese garrison held out until the end of the war.

A Type 95 *Ha-Go* captured on Guam. On 21 July 1944 the Japanese lost ten of these to Sherman and Bazooka fire. The Type 95 was to have been replaced by the Type 98 light tank in 1942, but very few were produced. Around 1,250 *Ha-Go*s were built; up-gunned variants included the Type 3 and Type 4, armed with a 57mm and 47mm gun respectively.

US Marines offer their thanks to the US Coastguard for their support at Guam. Note the Landing Vehicle Tracked (LVT) Water Buffalo behind them which were used extensively in the island-hopping campaigns in the Pacific.

Marine LVT Battalion officers who played a key role in the landings on Guam.

Chapter Eight

Pacific Victory

The M4 Sherman medium tank was used extensively by the US Army and the US Marine Corps from late 1943 onwards, and was involved in almost every island-hopping battle fought in the Pacific. The Sherman was vulnerable to the Japanese 47mm anti-tank gun that could penetrate the tank's side armour. To counter this threat, the crews made various field modifications using spare track blocks, bogey wheels, oak planks and sandbags. The frontal armour, in contrast, could withstand such punishment. The 47mm Type 1 anti-tank gun was the most modern in the Japanese inventory, but retained the driven trail spades that had hampered the manoeuvrability of the previous 37mm. While it could penetrate the side armour of American medium tanks, the small bursting charge inside the round often failed to explode.

Serving as a driver in a Sherman equipped with a dozer blade, Nile E. Darling, a USMC tanker, recalled:

> We took a direct hit from an enemy 47mm anti-tank gun. It hit the front slope plate of the tank and right in front of me. Since they were using smokeless powder and leaving no dust, we had trouble spotting their emplacement. My tank commander gave me the order to put the tank into reverse gear, my hand on my lap and not touch the brake lever, which I did and we backed up a few feet and then they hit us again. We then moved straight forward a few feet and they hit us a third time. We took five hits – none of which penetrated – before we could locate their gun and destroy it.

The Japanese garrisons in the Pacific turned every island they occupied into a fortress defended by mines, barbed wire, bunkers, pillboxes, weapons pits, tank traps, trenches, anti-tank guns and heavy artillery. The beaches were sown with mines and artillery shells and littered with obstacles. On the larger islands they also burrowed into and fortified the inland hills and mountains to create stop points and bunker networks from where they could continue to resist. Umurbrogol Mountain on Peleliu and Mount Suribachi on Iwo Jima were prime examples of this. Under such conditions the Stuart and Sherman's role was to help the troops get off the beaches and engage enemy strongpoints.

During the attack on Guadalcanal, the amphibious Landing Vehicle Tracked (LVT) or Amtrac was mainly used for logistical support. The development of the LVT-4 allowed for disembarkation by a rear ramp which greatly enhanced its combat utility. It was bloodied in this second role during the amphibious assault on Tarawa when 125 were committed to the attack. They were to ferry men across the coral reef and through the shallows to the beach.

At Tarawa on 20 November 1943, the Marines found that the tide had not risen sufficiently to clear the reef when they assaulted the island as part of Operation Galvanic. Only the LVTs got over, leaving the landing craft stranded. On the way in, the LVTs suffered from the intense Japanese fire and those that made it ashore were unable to clear the log sea wall. The return trip to the reef proved equally hazardous. As a result, only 35 remained operational by the end of the opening day of the invasion.

Similarly, the tank landing craft were hampered by the reef and suffered in the lagoon. On the east end of the beach two Stuart light tanks got ashore only to be knocked out. Six Shermans disembarked from their landing craft and climbed over the reef to be guided ashore by Marines on foot. Several were lost in sink holes and their engines drowned, but those reaching the western end of the island pushed forward to 270m in from the shore. One became stranded in a tank trap, while another detonated a magnetic mine. A third tank had its 75mm gun damaged by an incoming Japanese shell, so acted as a mobile pillbox. Four further tanks came ashore at noon, by which time the Marines had secured the beach up to the first line of Japanese defences. By the end of the day only one tank remained in action.

In the mid-afternoon the Japanese garrison commander ordered two Type 95s to cover his withdrawal from the concrete command post at the western end of the airfield. As he and his men gathered outside the bunker, American naval gunfire landed in their midst and killed them all.

As a result of the lessons learned at Tarawa, it was very evident that the LVT was too lightly armoured and too poorly armed. Some were converted into 'Amtanks' – amphibious tanks – armed with a 37mm gun or 75mm howitzer mounted in the M3 light tank turret to provide close fire support. LVTs subsequently played a key role in the Leyete landings and the Battle of Okinawa.

After the Marines came ashore on Guam either side of the Orote Peninsula on 21 July 1944, those on the northern beach met stiff resistance until the arrival of the tanks improved the situation. On the southern beach the Japanese counter-attacked around Hill 40 on numerous occasions. The attacks, resulting in heavy Japanese casualties, were supported by four Type 95 *Ha-Go* tanks which were easily destroyed by the Marines' bazookas or Shermans. In total the Japanese were to lose ten Type 95s on Guam. General Takashina, the garrison commander, was killed by machine-gun fire from a Sherman as he was overseeing the withdrawal in the Fonte area. Shermans of the 3rd Marine Tank Battalion were also involved in the fighting around Agana, east of the northern beachhead.

The amphibious assault on Peleliu Island on 15 September 1944 was the first time that the US Marines had armoured support for a landing. The plan was that the waterproofed Sherman tanks of the 1st Tank Battalion would disembark from their landing craft half a mile from the beach and cross the shallow waters while providing close gunfire support. The presence of a reef around the island meant that the Marines' Amtracs had to conduct a very exposed ferry service from the reef.

The right-hand brigade was allocated six Shermans, nine to the one in the centre and 15 to the left-hand brigade. The other 16 of the US 1st Marine Division's 46 tanks had to be left behind due to lack of shipping space. The well-dug-in Japanese garrison numbered 11,000 veteran troops, supported by the Type 95 *Ha-Go* light tanks armed with a 37mm gun (other sources state they were tiny two-man light Type 94 tankettes – either way they were wholly inadequate).

Within minutes of the first waves hitting the beach, 26 Amtracs were hit by accurate Japanese artillery and mortar fire. Some of these were carrying the assault force's communications equipment. The fourth wave included some 30 waterproofed tanks that waded ashore in six columns of five tanks each led by an Amtrac. Japanese artillery and mortar fire was so intense that 17 of the tanks were hit up to four times each, though only three were lost before reaching the beach. The Japanese responded to the invasion by launching a counter-attack across Peleliu airfield with up to 19 tanks. In an effort to close with the Marines as quickly as possible, the tanks quickly left behind the assaulting infantry.

Marine Robert Leckie was caught right in the firing line: 'Their tanks swooped suddenly upon us. They came tearing across the airfield, a dozen or so of them. It was startling. They came out of nowhere, and here were only riflemen and machine gunners to oppose them.' Leckie and his comrades were trapped in a bomb crater as 'The enemy tanks whizzed past, their little wheels whirling within their tracks.'

The 75mm guns of three Shermans, 37mm anti-tank guns, bazookas and anti-tank grenades met the Japanese tanks. One Marine said: 'A tank rushed for the machine-gun on my right. "Stoney" stands up in his foxhole (he's a lad with guts) and lets go a burst of automatic fire. The tank was not ten foot away when it burst into flame, leaving a trailing fire as it still rolled forward.' The vehicle forced the machine-gunners to flee for their lives as the burning tank rolled over their position and crushed their weapon.

When the Japanese tanks were approximately halfway across the airfield, four

Shermans appeared to the south. The US Marine Corps tankers found that their armour-piercing rounds went straight through the tanks' thin armour, so resorted to using high-explosive which blew them apart.

While the Marines opened up with everything they had, a US Navy dive-bomber also swooped in and dropped a bomb. Taking up the story again Leckie recalls: 'Once a torpedo plane flashed by, so low its belly might have scraped the coral. To my right, I saw a line of our tanks advancing, firing as they came, seeming to stop each time their guns stuttered. Then it was over.'

Corpsman Jack McCombs witnessed a bazooka team destroy one of the attacking force: 'A Jap was cut in half by machine-gun fire as he tried to get out of his tank. As a joke the guys carried his pants with the parts of his legs in them and threw them to one another. I know it sounds gruesome but it helped break the tension.'

Marine Eugene Sledge recorded the change in Japanese tactics: 'Rather than a banzai, the Japanese counterthrust turned out to be a well-coordinated tank–infantry attack. Approximately one company of Japanese infantry, together with about thirteen tanks, had moved carefully across the airfield until annihilated by the Marines on our left. This was our first warning that the Japanese might fight differently than they had elsewhere.'

In fact the Battle of Saipan, fought in June 1944, saw the largest Japanese tank battle of the Pacific War when the Japanese committed a much larger number of Type 97 medium tanks and Type 95 light tanks. Likewise the Battle of Okinawa, fought in the first half of 1945, saw the Japanese commit just under 30 tanks.

As the situation deteriorated for the Japanese in the Pacific in April 1944, the 9th Armored Regiment of the Japanese 1st Tank Division was reassigned to 31st Army, and dispatched to Saipan, where it was annihilated at the subsequent Battle of Saipan and Battle of Guam. Its remaining three regiments participated in Operation Ichi-Go on mainland China. The remaining units of the 2nd Tank Division were reassigned to the Japanese Fourteenth Area Army, and sent to the Philippines in July 1944. They were annihilated at the subsequent Battle of the Philippines.

For the invasion of Okinawa in April 1945, Lieutenant Colonel Bob Denig commanded the 6th Tank Battalion trained to provide divisional-level support rather than regimental. This was on the grounds that when a regiment was in reserve, the attached tank company was left kicking its heels.

By late May Denig noted:

The main thing about the show so far is the anti-defenses that the Nips have set up against the tanks. Their mainstay is the 47mm gun but we are [devising] and have devised means to take most of the sting out of it. The next worry are the mines and those jokers have put them all over the place. We have run over about 25 of them but only one tank was destroyed because of a mine. The remainder just blew off the track or something and we fix them up when we can work on them without fear of artillery fire. The Nips even shoot single 150mm guns at the tanks, sniping at them if you will. So far they have only hit one and that was on the front slope where it is thick and only one man was wounded and they drove the tank away and back to the park.

Terrain in the Pacific ensured that the M3/M5 light tanks remained of help throughout the war. Due to the poor types of anti-tank weapon possessed by the Japanese and the geography of the islands such as New Guinea, the small size and manoeuvrability of the American light tanks was often more important than heavier armour and more powerful armament.

A Japanese Type 97 medium tank knocked out on Saipan, which was assaulted on 15 June 1944. The Japanese tank force on Saipan included the modified Type 97 *Kai Shinhoto Chi-Ha*, armed with the high-velocity 47mm gun. During the battle, 36 Type 97s of the Japanese 9th Tank Regiment plus Type 95s from the 136th Infantry Regiment counter-attacked the US 6th Marine Regiment. This made it the largest Japanese tank action of the Pacific War.

These American LVT2(A) are bound for the beaches of Tinian island on 24 July 1944. In taking Tinian, US forces destroyed seven Type 95s that were supporting the Japanese garrison. The US Marine Corps also encountered dug-in Type 97 *Chi-Ha* tanks.

A column of 15 American Water Buffalo gathered for the invasion of Cape Sansapor, Dutch New Guinea, in 1944. They appear to be LVT(A)1 with the M3 turret mounting a 37mm gun.

A US M8 armoured car at Labiranan Head, Leyte, during the battle for Catmon Hill, 21 October 1944.

A selection of LVT(A)2, LVT4 and LVT(A)4s on the beaches of Iwo Jima in February 1945. The latter is distinguishable by the M8 motor carriage turret with the 75mm howitzer.

On Iwo Jima, naval guns, fighter-bombers and artillery were the gods of war. Amid the black sands of the island, gunners of the US 4th Marine Division fire their 105mm howitzer at Japanese targets.

Men of G Company, 24 Marine Regiment, take a break while supporting Shermans dealt with Japanese pillboxes between airfields 1 and 2 on Iwo Jima.

A US 37mm anti-tank gun engaging Japanese positions on Mount Suribachi, Iwo Jima. This volcanic mountain formed the heart of the Japanese defences on the island.

Men of the US 6th Marine Division destroying Japanese caves on Okinawa in May 1945.

A Sherman of the US 775th Tank Battalion engaging Japanese troops on Luzon in the Philippines in early 1945. The tank is covered in personal equipment including what looks like a Bazooka on the rear hull deck.

104

Chapter Nine

Jungles of Burma

Once Malaya was captured and Thailand occupied, the Japanese then set their sights on Burma. General Iida, commanding the Japanese Fifteenth Army, concentrated 100,000 men on the Thai border ready to invade Burma and cut off China's supply route from Rangoon. The British garrison consisted of an understrength division, the 1st Burma, which was reinforced in January 1942 by the arrival of the 17th Indian Division.

Burma was certainly not ideal tank country by any stretch of the imagination. As big as France and Belgium combined from north to south, it is dominated by a series of mountain ranges stretching from the Himalayas as well as two mighty rivers. To the west a range cuts Burma from India and stretches from upper Assam to the sea. Another spur, the Arakan Yomas, runs parallel with the coast almost as far south as Rangoon. From the west this range is shadowed by the Chindwin and Irrawaddy Rivers. These combine south of Mandalay and run through Magwe and Prome to Rangoon. Further east are the Sittang and Salween River valleys that lead up into the hills of the eastern Shan states and Yunnan in China.

The lack of metalled roads and the primitive railway ensured that the river valleys dominated all military movements. Burma's weather likewise severely hampered military operations. The monsoon season commences in mid-May and lasts through to October, bringing with it up to 800in of rain. This swells the rivers and turns the jungles into muddy swamps. Such a setting provided a fertile breeding ground for cholera, dysentery, malaria and typhus. Under such conditions the fighting tended to grind to a halt during the monsoon.

Following Pearl Harbor, America began to supply China with tanks including M3 Stuarts, and later M4 Shermans and M18 Hellcats, which trickled in through Burma and formed part of several well-equipped, well-trained armies. An estimated 812 Shermans were shipped to China under Lend-Lease, while Chinese forces in India received 100 M4A4 Shermans and employed them to some effect in the subsequent 1943 and 1944 offensives.

In the meantime, when the Japanese attack came on 15 January 1942, the only other troops available were the British 7th Armoured Brigade and a single Chinese division. In February the Japanese landed troops in Rangoon from the sea creating a critical situation for the Allies. In the face of a two-pronged Japanese attack, British forces deployed in Burma had little choice but to conduct a fighting withdrawal northwards.

The Japanese intention was to protect their southern flank in Malaya, grab Burma's oilfields and sever Chiang Kai-Shek's supply route, thereby weakening his war effort. To prevent this, Chinese forces were committed to help bolster the weak British position. During February, from Yunnan province in western China, troops under General Luo Chuoying moved into southern Burma down the main road to Lashio, Mandalay, Meiktila and then Toungoo (also spelled Taungoo).

The Chinese Expeditionary Force in Burma consisted of three armies – the 5th (under General Du Yuming), 6th and 66th. The first two, ironically partly trained and equipped by Germany, were considered among Chiang's best. Certainly the 5th Army was the only one that had any field guns.

General Sir William Slim, the Burma Corps commander, observed that a Chinese Army actually only corresponded to a European corps of two or three divisions. He also noted:

> The rifle power of a Chinese division at full strength rarely exceeded three thousand, with a couple of hundred light machine guns, thirty or forty medium machine guns, and a few three inch mortars. There were no artillery units except a very occasional anti-tank gun of small calibre, no medical services, meagre signals, a staff car or two, half a dozen trucks, and a couple of hundred shaggy, ill-kept ponies.

In other words, exactly the sort of Chinese fighting force the Japanese expected to encounter.

Crucially the Chinese lacked vital armoured and mechanised forces that could act as a mobile reserve and counter Japanese breakthroughs. They only had a single 'armoured' unit, designated the 200th Motorised Infantry Division (which until the late 1930s had been a mechanised division), and supporting tank battalions. In some histories the 200th Division has been described as an armoured division, but this was far from the case.

Generalissimo Chiang Kai-shek, in part to ensure continued material support from Washington, subordinated these forces to an American general. Much to the senior Chinese commander General Luo Chuoying's displeasure, they came under the command of General Joseph W. Stillwell, who was known as 'Vinegar Joe' because of his abrasive manner. The idea was that General Luo would take orders from Stilwell, while all the other commanders took orders from Luo. Such an arrangement inevitably led to friction and resentment.

Stilwell was suspicious that Chiang was playing a duplicitous game. He hoped American equipment supplied under Lend-Lease via Rangoon would equip 30 Chinese divisions to fight the Japanese in Burma. Instead Chiang was more intent on using it to shore up his political position by parcelling the equipment out to his 300 divisional commanders scattered across Nationalist-held China. Many of the generals commanded little more than local militias that had no intention of tangling with the Japanese either in Burma or China.

In addition Chiang was planning a long game and stockpiling much of his supplies ready to fight the Communists in northern China. On top of this, much of the material of war gathered at Lashio was siphoned off before it ever reached Chiang's capital at Chungking. When Stilwell arrived in Chungking there was no sign of his much-hoped-for 30 divisions.

At the end of January 1942 it was agreed that the Chinese 5th Army would take over the Toungoo area in the Sittang Valley to the north-east of Rangoon. This would permit the transfer of the 1st Burma Division across the Irrawaddy Valley to join the 17th Indian Division. In the event, only the 200th Division reached Toungoo. Under the command of Major-General Dai Anlan, it included a motorised cavalry regiment and three infantry regiments. He set about establishing defensive positions in and around the town, but crucially was left unsupported.

Stilwell urgently wanted three Chinese divisions to reinforce the 200th. However, it was to be a sacrificial lamb to Chinese politics. The three divisional commanders, under instruction from Chiang Kai-Shek, used every trick in the book to delay their units' move to the front. Stilwell, never one to mince his words, was so furious that he branded the Chinese generals 'pusillanimous bastards'. Chiang's real purpose was to ensure that the Japanese pushed north towards India and did not swing east into China. He had no intention of losing his best forces defending Burma for the British.

Major-General Dai Anlan fought two Japanese divisions at Toungoo in March 1942. Despite determined resistance, by the end of the month his beleaguered 200th Division had suffered 3,000 casualties (from a strength of about 7,000 men) and was surrounded. They had done a professional and highly competent job of holding the Japanese at bay, but without help were doomed. The survivors were forced to abandon their vehicles and heavy equipment in order to break out of the Japanese cordon. Although reinforcements from another Chinese division reached the area, they could do little but cover the retreat. It was a sorry end to the Chinese expeditionary force's only motorised division.

Stilwell noted of the Chinese tank battalion: 'They are green men in the military sense, and many of them have come from China's paddy fields to drive a motor driven vehicle for the first time in their lives.' He went on to praise its performance in the Hukawng Valley later.

Meanwhile, in trying to alleviate the pressure at Toungoo, the 17th Indian Division was ordered to counter-attack. Three infantry battalions supported by a squadron of tanks and a battery of guns were sent to drive back the Japanese. Instead, this force was surrounded at the village of Schwedaung 50 miles west of Toungoo. They broke out but not before losing their vehicles, tanks and guns.

The Chinese Expeditionary Force under Stilwell then moved to save the encircled British troops at the Yenangyaung oilfields to the north-west of Toungoo. The Japanese 33rd Division had managed to trap two British brigades and a tank battalion, so Stilwell rushed a single Chinese division to the rescue. Under Lieutenant General Sun Li-jen, the Chinese 38th Division, along with the British 7th Armoured Brigade, was sent to rescue the 1st Burma Division at Yenangyaung. Slim was highly impressed by General Sun and noted: 'He was, as far as I know, the first Chinese general to have the artillery and armoured units of an ally placed actually under his command....'. Together they fought for four days to free the Burma Division.

On 17–18 April, after a 48-hour battle, the Japanese were defeated and 7,000 British and Indian troops were saved from capture. 'I was, I confess, surprised at how he [the Chinese soldier] had responded to the stimulus of proper tank and artillery support, and at the aggressive spirit he had shown. I had never expected, either, to get a Chinese general of the calibre of Sun,' Slim recalled in his memoirs of the fighting at Yenangyaung.

The absence of this Chinese division came at a price and left the right wing of Stilwell's main forces exposed; the Japanese were swift to exploit this weakness and drove the Chinese back. The Japanese seized Lashio, in the Chinese rear, cutting the vital road link to the border. By June 1942 the Japanese were in control of all of Burma with the British in headlong retreat back into India. Part of the Chinese Expeditionary Force under General Sun also retreated into India to reorganise while the main force withdrew to western Yunnan province to re-equip.

Thanks to superior equipment, a superior air force and unified strategy, the Japanese, with ten infantry divisions and two armoured battalions, were able to defeat the combined forces of China, Britain, India and Burma and cut international communications to China in a single campaign. They lost 1,200 men killed and over 3,000 wounded, while Chinese losses alone exceeded 10,000. The loss of the Generalissimo's two best armies in Burma deprived China of over a third of her strategic reserve and was to have ramifications elsewhere. What was evident was that the lack of mechanised and motorised forces cost the Allies dearly in Burma. It was a lesson they would not ignore.

General Sun Li-jen led the Chinese 38th Division in Burma and then became the commander of the Chinese Army in India following the retreat. Lacking armour and artillery, the 38th had to be bolstered by British tanks in 1942, nonetheless General Slim thought highly of its competent commander.

A Chinese boy soldier serving with the three divisions of X Force which retreated into India from Burma. General Sun's remaining troops were reinforced with 13,000 men flown in from China. They were re-equipped and trained by US and British instructors and their equipment included limited numbers of light and medium tanks. Those Chinese units operating out of Yunnan, China, were known as Y Force.

American supply trucks heading for China. Once the Japanese had cut the Burma Road, the Allies created the Ledo Road in 1944, running from Assam in India to China.

Burma was more suited to irregular rather than mechanised warfare. The Chindits, formed from the 77th Indian Infantry Brigade and men of the King's Liverpool Regiment, conducted guerrilla warfare behind Japanese lines in India and Burma during 1943 and 1944.

General Stilwell with General Frank Merrill in Burma. Merrill was another proponent of guerrilla warfare and led the US special forces, dubbed 'Merrill's Marauders', in Burma during 1944.

Cheerful-looking Indian troops photographed in Burma in 1944. Their weapons include Enfield rifles, a Bren light machine-gun and a Thompson sub-machine-gun.

M3 Lee medium tanks supporting the Gurkhas during the Battle of Imphal. This operation involved the 254th Indian Tank Brigade equipped with Lee, Sherman and Stuart tanks.

An RAF Hawker Hurricane supporting the ground forces during the Imphal-Kohima fighting.

A British Sherman tank commander and his Indian crew from the 255th Indian Tank Brigade take a break from the fighting at Meiktila for a bit of sightseeing. During the battle, General Slim's mechanised forces proved their worth by trapping and overwhelming the Japanese garrison.

Chinese-crewed Shermans photographed on the Burma Road in 1945. Initially the Chinese were supplied with M2A4 light tanks, which were followed by M3A3 and M5A1 Stuart light tanks and M4A4 Sherman medium tanks during 1943 and 1944. However, the numbers involved were relatively small.

A column of Chinese M3A3 or M5A1 light tanks involved in the fighting at Bhamo, Burma in 1944. The two crewmen in the foreground are wearing the US Model 1938 tanker's helmet and are armed with Thompson sub-machine-guns.

British M3 Grants operating in Burma. This tank proved to be the workhorse of the British and Indian armoured units and served each of them well.

Chapter Ten

Assault on India

When General Sir William Slim was appointed Corps commander in Burma in early 1942, on inspecting the 7th Armoured Brigade he was not altogether pleased.

Its two regiments of light tanks, American Stuarts or Honeys, mounting as they did only a two-pounder [37mm] gun and having very thin armour which any anti-tank weapon would pierce, were by no means ideal for the sort of close fighting the terrain required. Any weakness in the tanks, however, was made up by their crews. The 7th Hussars and 2nd Royal Tank Regiment were as good British troops as I had seen anywhere. They had had plenty of fighting in the Western Desert before coming to Burma and they looked what they were – confident, experienced, tough soldiers.

Slim himself had no experience of fighting with an armoured brigade. During the retreat through Burma he and his commanders tended to use their tanks in penny packets with widely dispersed detachments of infantry. They saw the dispersal of tanks as good for the morale of the latter, rather than being of any sound tactical logic.

Once the British Army deployed the Sherman in North Africa it despatched around 1,700 M3 General Grant/Lee medium tanks to fight in the war in South-East Asia. This tank had served as a welcome stop-gap in North Africa, having greater punch than British tank designs, but proved less popular with the Russians who were already fielding the vastly superior T-34 medium tank.

Indian forces were equipped with 900 M3s, while the Australians received 800. British Army Lee and Grant tanks served with the British 14th Army from the fall of Rangoon until the very end of the war. The M3 was not used as a tank-to-tank weapon but rather in an infantry support role. Although it had a poor off-road capability, it performed remarkably well in the hilly terrain of the region.

A British counter-attack was launched from Chittagong in September 1942 by the 14th Indian Division along the Arakan coastal region, but their advance was delayed by the weather as well as by training and supply problems. Early in 1943 the offensive was halted and in April the Japanese counter-attacked, driving the division back to its starting point. The British launched their second Arakan offensive in December 1943 employing the 5th and 7th Indian Divisions. They were also halted by strong Japanese positions and were cut off by a counter-offensive. An attack by the 26th Indian Division forced the Japanese to retreat, failing in their aim of diverting more British troops from the Imphal area.

Throughout 1944 and into early 1945 the Japanese Army's meagre tank forces fared very poorly. In contrast, the Indian Army's tank brigades fought bravely with their superior armour. The Battle of Imphal in the spring and summer of 1944 involved the 254th Indian Tank Brigade, equipped with Lee, Sherman and Stuart tanks. All of these were more than capable of dealing with the lightly armoured Japanese tanks.

The bulk of the British 14th Army's IV Corps holding Imphal in north-east India was made up of Indian Army infantry divisions comprising Indian, British and Gurkha troops. The jungle covering the hills around Kohima was far from ideal tank country. Beyond these, mountains blocked the way to Imphal. The latter provided ideal defensive positions for the Japanese. In addition many of the battles around Imphal were fought during the monsoon season.

Supporting the Japanese Yamamoto Force, the main armoured unit was the 14th Tank Regiment with 66 tanks (comprising the Japanese Type 95 *Ha-Go* light tank and captured British M3 Stuart light tanks). Six Type 95 *Ha-Go* tanks encountered six M3 Lee tanks from the 3rd Carabiniers on 20 March 1944 with the Japanese armour succumbing swiftly to the Lees' vastly superior firepower.

The following month the Japanese attacked up the main road from Tamu to Imphal. Lacking timely infantry support, British anti-tank guns claimed 12 Japanese tanks exposed on the road. On 13 April Lee tanks helped drive the Japanese from the Nungshigum Ridge that overlooked the main airstrip at Imphal. The Japanese defenders were shocked when the brave tank crews drove their vehicles up the very steep incline, which the Japanese assumed was impassable to armour.

At the same time the Japanese attacked Kohima, also in north-east India. Their objective was the Kohima Ridge which dominated the road along which supplies were ferried to the British and Indian troops of IV Corps at Imphal. By the time the Japanese broke off from the Battle of Imphal and Kohima they had lost 55,000 casualties including 13,500 dead. Many of these losses were due to starvation and disease.

Under such conditions a single tank could make all the difference to the outcome of an engagement. This proved to be the case during the fighting at Kohima, clearing the Japanese from the area of the District Commissioner's bungalow on Garrison Hill, which they had been holding since early April. The 2nd Dorsets had been unable to surround the enemy positions and what was needed was some close-support heavy firepower on the ground overlooking the Japanese. Artillery was considered too indiscriminate because of the closeness of the frontlines. As Colonel O.G.W. White DSO, the 2nd Dorsets' commanding officer, so eloquently put it: 'if we could only get a medium tank on to the tennis court, serving some pretty fast balls from the north end, the Nip would not stay to finish the set'.

On the morning of 28 April 1944 a Royal Engineers bulldozer, with a Lee M3 medium tank in front and one behind, rumbled up the Manipur road and began to clear a track up the steep hill. Once the bulldozer had completed this task it tried to drag one of the tanks up the slope, the end result was that the tank pulled the bulldozer on top of it and both crashed down the rest of the slope. They tried again on 4 May and managed to get a tank into the District Commissioner's compound, but it could not reach the tennis court higher up. Eight days later the engineers bulldozed a path straight up Garrison Hill spur.

On 13 May Sergeant J. Waterhouse of the 149th Royal Armoured Corps Regiment, supported by infantry, slid his M3 medium tank into the middle of the tennis court and crushed one of the enemy's main defensive positions. Waterhouse recalled:

> We pulled to the right and found ourselves in front of a steel water tank very heavily sandbagged and small arms fire met us. My 75mm gunner dealt with this position so effectively that the Nips started to leave in hell of a hurry without even arms and equipment ... We next paid our attention to a series of crawl trenches and machine-gun posts all around the court, and had hell of a party for the next 20 minutes or so ... The whole action lasted about 40 minutes and the infantry suffered only one casualty and even he walked out.

Under increasing pressure, the Japanese plan was that the 15th Army would withdraw beyond the Irrawaddy River, which would hold the Allies at bay. At the same time, to the east, the 33rd Army would carry on holding up the Americans and Chinese attempting to open a land route from India to China. Likewise, to the west, the 28th Army would hold the coastal Arakan Province using the terrain to slow the Allies.

Crucially the Japanese forces were woefully understrength and lacked adequate anti-tank weapons with which to stem the tide of Allied tanks. All they could do was deploy their field artillery in a direct-fire role against the enemy armour, but in doing so this deprived the infantry of indirect fire support. The expedient of using explosive suicide vests or explosive charges on a long pole (lunge mines) was only effective if the enemy tanks were not supported by infantry.

General Slim recalled a desperate anti-tank measure adopted by his enemies:

A Japanese soldier with a 100-kilo aircraft bomb between his knees, holding a large stone, poised above the fuse would crouch in a foxhole. When the attacking tank passed over the almost invisible hole, he would drop the stone – then bomb, man, and, it was hoped, tank would all go up together. Luckily the device was not very effective and accounted for more Japanese than tanks.

In December 1944 the third Arakan offensive was launched by the 25th Indian and 82nd West African Divisions and on this occasion the Japanese coastal airfields were taken. At the same time, the 14th Army under Slim crossed the Chindwin and marched on the Irrawaddy. In a brilliant piece of deception, Slim convinced the enemy his main crossing would be near Mandalay but instead he chose Meiktila. The sole Japanese tank unit supporting just under a dozen Japanese divisions was the battered 14th Tank Regiment which by 1945 only had 20 tanks.

During February 1945 the 255th Indian Tank Brigade, equipped with Shermans, fought in the Battle of Pokoku and Irrawaddy River operations supporting the 17th Indian Infantry Division forming part of IV Corps. During the crossing of the Irrawaddy by the 14th Army, which saw Grant tanks ferried over on pontoons, opposing Japanese tanks and guns fell victim to circling Allied fighter-bombers. Meanwhile the XXXIII Corps was supported by the 254th Indian Tank Brigade.

The Japanese were finally defeated during the concurrent battles of Meiktila and Mandalay in early 1945. Meiktila proved to be a tough but ultimately highly successful battle for Slim, in which mechanised forces proved their worth. Victory was far from guaranteed as the Japanese, under Major-General Kasuya, numbered around 12,000 men in the Meiktila area, while in the town itself the well-equipped and dug-in garrison totalled some 3,200. Japanese defences extended in an oval around 3 miles by 4 miles with two large lakes protecting those positions to the north-west and south-west. They had a considerable number of heavy weaponry, including anti-aircraft guns deployed for anti-tank and perimeter defence.

At the beginning of March 1945 it fell to the 255th Indian Tank Brigade to ensure that the Japanese were cut off at Meiktila. It was also tasked with taking the airfield to the east of the town. Supported by a self-propelled 25-pounder battery and two infantry battalions, the brigade's tanks swung north-east and then westward in behind the Japanese. Slim recalled: 'This armoured onrush was met by very heavy artillery, anti-tank, and machine-gun fire from a deep screen of mutually supporting bunkers and fortified houses.'

Close to the south-eastern corner of Meiktila the 255th Tank Brigade attacked a steep hill that rose for over 500ft at the edge of South Lake. Although heavily defended, once the brigade had secured it the hill gave them a clear view over the entire area.

At the same time, the 63rd Brigade moved to the west to set up blocking positions in an area unsuitable for vehicles, while 48th Brigade attacked from the north skirting around Meiktila Lake. Slim, who visited the battle, witnessed an Indian manned Sherman tank supporting Gurkhas of the 48th Brigade attacking Japanese bunkers with great effect. The garrison resisted to the bitter end with their 75mm field guns engaging enemy tanks and infantry at point-blank range.

By the end of 3 March Meiktila had been captured, followed by its vital airfield. In some desperation the Japanese attempted to counter-attack with elements from seven different divisions. Although the fighting continued until the end of March, these forces were defeated piecemeal as they tried to converge by air attacks and aggressive armoured fighting columns. Wherever they were located, the Japanese were destroyed.

The tanks of Major-General T.W. Rees's 19th Indian Division overwhelmed Japanese defences north of Mandalay by 4 March. A motorised column then seized Madaya the following day and three days later was pressing on the city's northern outskirts. At Mandalay, artillery and air power – not tanks – were the key to victory as the defenders had to be blasted from Fort Dufferin.

Just to the west, once across the Irrawaddy, the 20th Indian Division were keeping up the pressure thrusting south. Notably the 100th Brigade, spearheaded by an armoured and motorised column, was tasked with linking up with IV Corps at Meiktila. On 21 March 1945 it reached Wundwin, between Mandalay and Meiktila, which was held by administrative elements of the Japanese 18th Division. Once the town was captured the brigade then struck north destroying a few light tanks and capturing guns and lorries as well as a solitary enemy tank.

In the face of this concerted attack, the exhausted Japanese abandoned Rangoon and withdrew towards Thailand. Japan finally surrendered in mid-August, while the Japanese troops in China, excluding Manchuria, formally surrendered on 9 September 1945.

A 25-pounder crew in action at Pinwe, Burma, with the 36th Indian Division on 20 November 1944.

A British 3.7in mountain howitzer providing support to the advancing troops and tanks in Burma in November 1944.

An Indian mountain battery moving up from the Ramree landing, 16 February 1945. British forces first landed on this Japanese-held island off the Burmese coast on 21 January 1945.

Shermans and lorries of the 63rd Motorised Brigade advancing from Nyaungyu on Meiktila in March 1945.

A British M3 Lee medium tank, belonging to 2nd Division, being loaded onto a ferry ready to cross the Irrawaddy at Ngazun, 28 February 1945.

Admiral Lord Louis Mountbatten, Supreme Allied Commander South-East Asia, sits astride a captured Japanese Type 38 75mm gun while addressing men of the Royal Armoured Corps in liberated Mandalay, 21 March 1945.

Troops of the 15th Indian Corps disembarking their 25-pounder guns from landing craft at Elephant Point south of Rangoon, 2 May 1945.

A Stuart light tank belonging to an Indian cavalry regiment pushing on Rangoon, April 1945.

Australian gunners with a 25-pounder Short Mark I. Designed for jungle warfare, this first appeared in 1943 and was deployed by the Australian Army during the New Guinea Campaign.

British troops in Burma in 1945 with a Japanese 37mm anti-tank gun. This looks to be the later Type 1. During the 1930s the Japanese military drew the wrong conclusions about its requirement for tanks and anti-tank weapons – as a result it never caught up during the Second World War.

This British Universal carrier, converted into a light tank by the Japanese, was recaptured in Java in 1945.

Chapter Eleven

August Storm

By 1945 the Japanese Kwantung forces in Manchuria (or Manchukuo) included the 1st and 3rd Armies, with the 4th in the far north. On paper the powerful Kwantung Army could field 600,000 men in 25 divisions equipped with 1,215 armoured cars and light tanks, 6,700 pieces of artillery and 1,800 aircraft (of which just 50 were frontline); they were supported by eight wholly inadequate divisions of the Chinese Manchukuo Forces numbering 40,000 men.

Although Japan intended to hold Manchuria, because of its industry and raw materials, the Japanese Army was in no condition to do so. In reality the Kwantung Army was in a poor condition and only capable of policing duties. Although it could muster considerable manpower, it lacked the modern accoutrements of war. At this stage of the conflict it was firmly an infantry force. As the Second World War progressed, this once large, well-trained and well-equipped army could not be held in strategic reserve indefinitely.

In the closing years of the war many of its better frontline divisions were systematically stripped of their most experienced troops and best equipment, which were then scattered in the fighting against the Americans in the Pacific Islands and the Philippines. Notably its armoured formations were diverted to southern China, Korea and the Philippines, so the Kwantung Army was no longer able to conduct mechanised operations of any size. In particular many of its units were sent south into China to support Operation Ichi-Go during 1944–45.

The Japanese 12th Armoured Regiment, formerly based in Taiyuan, was withdrawn to bolster the defences of Seoul in Korea towards the closing stages of the war, and as part of the Japanese 17th Area Army was in combat against the Red Army's invasion of Manchuria. The 2nd Tank Division was reconstituted in Japan as a training unit after the disaster in the Philippines. In February 1945, its 11th Armoured Regiment was transferred to the control of the Japanese 5th Area Army and redesignated the 91st Division. It was stationed in the northern Kurile Islands, where it was in combat against the Red Army at Paramushir during the invasion of the Kurile Islands at the end of the Second World War. It was officially demobilised in September 1945, along with the rest of the Imperial Japanese Army.

The commander of the Kwantung, General Otozō Yamada, hastily tried to organise large numbers of poorly trained conscripts and 'volunteers' into eight new infantry divisions and seven new infantry brigades. The Kwantung's dubious Chinese allies, the Manchukuo Imperial Army, comprised eight infantry and seven cavalry divisions. In the face of a fully fledged mechanised offensive by the Red Army, the Japanese had little confidence that these Chinese troops would stand their ground. The Manchukuo forces must have known that their best prospect was to defect at the first opportunity or face being run over by a Soviet tank.

While the Japanese were anticipating a Russian attack at the end of the Second World War, they assessed it would not be until October 1945 or in the spring of the following year. Just three months after Nazi Germany surrendered, the Red Army invaded Manchukuo. The offensive was conducted between the two atomic bombs dropped on Hiroshima on 6 August and Nagasaki on 9 August 1945. The Russians avenged themselves for Khalkhin-Gol with Operation August Storm launched on 8 August.

The scale of this armoured assault was a vast repetition of Khalkhin-Gol, but this time the pincer movement enveloped an area the size of Western Europe. The Soviets threw about 80 divisions – totalling 1.5 million men, over 5,000 tanks, over 28,000 artillery pieces and 4,300 aircraft – at the Japanese. Perhaps predictably the fighting lasted less than a week before the Japanese declared a ceasefire.

The Soviet pincer movement from the east crossed the Ussuri River and advanced around Lake Khanka. It attacked towards Suifenhe, and although Japanese defenders fought hard and provided strong resistance, the Soviets proved overwhelming. After a week of fighting, during which Soviet forces had penetrated deep into Manchukuo, Japan's Emperor Hirohito recorded the *Gyokuon-hōsō* which was broadcast on radio to the Japanese nation on 15 August 1945. While it stated Japan would accept the terms of the Potsdam Declaration, it made no direct reference to surrender and pockets of fierce resistance from the Kwantung Army continued.

Although Yamada ordered the surrender the day after Emperor Hirohito's announcement, some Japanese divisions refused to lay down their arms and fighting went on for the next few days. On 18 August several Soviet amphibious landings were conducted ahead of the land advance: three in northern Korea, one in Sakhalin, and one in the Kurile Islands. The Soviets continued their advance, largely avoiding the pockets of resistance, reaching Mukden, Changchun and Qiqihar by 20 August.

Over half a million Japanese prisoners of war were sent to Soviet labour camps in Siberia, the Russian Far East and Mongolia. Japan's remaining armoured forces lay in ruins and few had any use for its obsolete tank designs. Nonetheless China deployed numbers of the Type 97 *Chi Ha* medium tank well after the war's end.

Japanese defences in Manchuria were under-resourced and concrete blockhouses such as this were few and far between.

The Japanese Type 88 75mm anti-aircraft gun could operate in a dual role as an anti-tank weapon and was effective against the Sherman in the Pacific. However, it was not very mobile, which made it vulnerable to Soviet artillery, tanks and fighter-bombers in Manchuria.

The Japanese Type 95, deployed with the Kwantung Army in Manchuria, was obsolete in comparison to the powerful tanks and tank destroyers of the Red Army.

The Japanese Army had few, if any, weapons capable of tackling the Soviet T-34/85 armed with a powerful 85mm anti-tank gun.

Red Army tank crews posing with their T-34/85 and SU-100 tank destroyer somewhere in the Far East.

Port Arthur – once more in Russian hands. The Soviet Navy's Pacific Fleet Marines hoisted the flag over the port on 1 October 1945, following the Red Army's invasion of Manchuria that crushed the Kwantung Army.

Chapter Twelve

Slow and Poorly Armed

Thanks to their experiences firstly in Manchuria in the 1930s and then Malaya and the Philippines in 1941–42, the Japanese saw little utility in massing their tanks or indeed their artillery. Both weapons were consigned to an infantry support role. The reason for this was that Chinese armies did not field tanks and at the first sign of artillery fire Chinese troops, especially warlord militias, tended to melt away. The Japanese found that using such weapons at a purely regimental level was sufficient. In Malaya the British authorities had declared the terrain as not fit for armoured warfare, so Japanese tank regiments encountered very little opposition. Likewise in the Philippines the Japanese were lulled into a false sense of security following their successful clashes with American light tanks.

Large concentrations of Japanese tanks were not encountered, so there were never any large-scale tank-to-tank battles in the same vein as those in North Africa, north-west Europe and on the Eastern Front. Only during the invasion of Malaya in 1941 and the Ichi-Go offensive of 1944 did Japanese tanks play any significant role in the fighting. The invasion of Malaya was supported by around 300 tanks from the Japanese 3rd Tank Division, which were largely tankettes and Type 95s. Numbers of these types were also sent to the Philippines to support the invasion there. Some of the newer up-armoured Type 1 *Chi-He*s were deployed to the Bataan Peninsula in 1943.

As a result, Allied armour likewise remained in the more traditional role of infantry support. The one exception was the race for Rangoon by the armoured units of the 14th Army, which is often referred to as one of the greatest pursuits in the history of British arms. This saw two tank brigades driving 'hell for leather' along the two main routes toward the capital, desperate to get there before the monsoon set in.

The Japanese also disadvantaged themselves because they remained wedded to the 37mm anti-tank gun throughout the Second World War. By 1939 every major nation recognised that the 37mm was no longer up to the job and had heavier anti-tank weapons on the drawing board. The Germans developed 50mm, 75mm and then 88mm guns, the Soviets 76.2mm and 85mm guns, while the Allies standardised at 75mm and 76mm. By 1942 most nations had dispensed with their 37mm and 45mm anti-tank guns. The Japanese, in an act of hubris, viewed their own tanks as the norm to be beaten and built guns capable of doing that, then considered this good enough to beat their enemies' tanks. This failure to move with the times inevitably cost them when their troops came up against British Matilda and American Grant and Sherman tanks.

During the Battle of Khalkhin-Gol in 1939, Zhukov quickly developed a poor opinion of Japanese tanks, branding them outdated. He recalled: 'They are slow, poorly armed and have very limited action radius.' The Japanese discovered that the Type 97's muzzle velocity was inadequate against Soviet armour and yet they failed to address this shortcoming with any sense of urgency. It was a technological decision that cost them dearly and remained largely unchanged until the very end of the war.

In Japan, the 4th Tank Division was created out of the training units of the Armour, Cavalry, Field Artillery and Military Engineering Schools of the Imperial Japanese Army Academy, plus the staff and students, on 6 July 1944. This was placed under the 36th Army and deployed for the defence of the Japanese home islands against the projected Allied invasion. It was not to see combat. The 1st Tank Division was reassigned to the Japanese home islands in March 1945, also in preparation for an expected invasion. It was bolstered by the 1st Armoured Regiment from the 3rd Tank Division, and also formed part of the 36th Army under the Japanese 12th Area Army.

Japan, by 1940, had produced just over 2,000 Type 95/97 light tanks and Type 97 medium tanks. Two years later Japanese tank production peaked at just 1,300, but fell to only 295 by 1944. At that stage, fighter aircraft were considered a far greater priority. These Japanese light and medium tanks were no match for their Allied counterparts. While later Japanese designs were better armed, they were built in such small numbers that they had little bearing on the subsequent fighting. This contrasts sharply with the tens of thousands of Shermans, T-34s and Panzer IVs that were churned out.

Likewise, the upgraded Japanese Type 1 37mm anti-tank gun was available only in limited quantities, and the additional barrel length provided for only an incremental improvement over the more numerous Type 94 37mm gun. Approximately 2,300 Type 1 37mm guns were produced, but given the size of the Imperial Japanese Army, this was clearly insufficient. It was marginally effective against the M3 Stuart light tank in the Pacific, but not against the M4 Sherman which was soon fielded in large numbers by the Allies. The Type 1 47mm anti-tank gun was accepted into service in 1942. The design originated as an improvement to the prototype 'Experimental Type 97 (1937) 47mm anti-tank gun', which was tested between 1938 and 1939.

The 47mm gun was introduced for combat only in 1943, and up until that time Japanese infantry had considerable difficulty even against the Allied M3 Stuart light tank in the Pacific. However, by the time the Type 1 was available in any quantities, the M3 had been superseded by the heavier M4 Sherman, against which it was only marginally effective if it hit the side armour.

The Type 97 20mm anti-tank rifle was quite useful in the early Pacific campaigns, but could not match the Allies' heavily armoured tanks, such as the Sherman. In 1942, having learnt about the German hollow charge anti-tank grenade, a copy subsequently slightly improved the performance of the Type 97 anti-tank rifle.

In part Japan was defeated in South-East Asia and the Pacific because it failed to adapt to armoured and mechanised warfare quickly enough. By the time it did realise the merits of powerful, mobile and concentrated armoured forces, the US Navy and Air Forces were pressing in on the Japanese homeland and tanks were a luxury the Japanese Imperial Army could no longer afford. In the case of the up-gunned tanks of the Japanese 4th Tank Division, it was too little too late and they were handed over to the US occupation forces without ever firing a shot.

American armour was not completely impervious to Japanese shellfire, as this turretless Sherman testifies.

Unlike Manchuria, Mongolia and even Burma, the Pacific Islands were singularly ill-suited for mechanised warfare – as this aerial intelligence photo of Betio Island, Tarawa Atoll, shows. Under such conditions, the Japanese defenders had few places to hide their tanks, especially in the face of US air superiority. At the same time, US Amtracs and Shermans crossing the shallows, were highly vulnerable to mines and artillery and mortar fire.

Japanese infantry killed during the New Guinea Campaign. The Japanese Army lacked tank support and what it did have was slow and poorly armed. As a result they increasingly relied on suicidal infantry attacks.

Marines taking a break from the fighting on Peleliu. Behind them can be seen an Amtrac. These, along with the Sherman, ensured the Marines got onto and across the invasion beaches.

American Landing Ships disgorging vehicles and supplies on Iwo Jima beach. In the face of such resources, the Imperial Japanese Army could not hope to win.

A Type 94 tankette captured during the Battle of Okinawa, which lasted from early April until mid-June 1945. This is the earlier model, also known as the Type 92, and is identifiable by its small rear-drive sprocket visible on the left.

A Type 95 in the hills around Shuri on Okinawa. The 800 American tanks committed to the invasion easily outnumbered the Japanese 27th Tank Regiment's 13 Type 95 and 14 Type 97 *Shinhoto* medium tanks.

US Marines passing a dead Japanese soldier on Okinawa in April 1945.

Brand new and unused Type 3 *Chi-Nu*s with the Japanese 4th Armoured Division. Armed with a Type 3 75mm tank gun, this tank was belatedly designed to take on the Sherman. By 1945 some six tank regiments were equipped with the *Chi-Nu*, including the 1st and 4th Tank Divisions guarding Tokyo. The Japanese surrender in August 1945 ensured they never saw action.

A US M7 self-propelled 105mm howitzer firing on Japanese positions at Catmon Hill, Leyte, 27 October 1944.

143

American GIs examining knocked-out Japanese tanks. The vehicle in the foreground appears to be a Type 95 *Ha-Go* light tank, while in front of it is a Type 89B medium tank. Judging by the position of the dead crew, they were caught in an ambush. Landings took place in the Philippines in January 1945; Manila was liberated the following month, but Luzon Island was not declared secure until July 1945. During the fighting ten Type 95s were destroyed on Leyte and another 19 on Luzon.

An M7 Priest self-propelled howitzer rolling into Cebu City, Philippines. The battle to liberate the city was fought in late March and early April 1945.

Type 95s belonging to the Japanese 16th Tank Regiment on Marcus Island. Although bombed, the island was never taken and did not surrender until the end of the war.